Simpler Times

Also by the Author

How to Build & Operate
Your Own Small Hydroelectric Plant

Simpler Times

Stories of Early Twentieth Century City Life

J. GEORGE BUTLER

VANDAMERE
PRESS

Published by
Vandamere Press
P.O. Box 5243
Arlington, VA 22205
USA

Copyright © 1997
Vandamere Press
ISBN 0-918339-25-1

Dedication

This book is dedicated to
the author's parents,
Helena J. and the Reverend Charles H. Butler,
who in spite of the stupidities of my youth,
taught me how to live.
To them I can never repay the debt I owe
for their wisdom, their patience, and
their sacrificial and loving care.

Acknowledgments

Without the encouragement and help of my publisher, Art Brown, who has seen this manuscript through many versions, this book would not have been possible. For Art's expertise, patience, and guidance I am deeply grateful. He has become a true friend.

I deeply appreciate Charles Kuralt's gracious foreword. Words cannot express my gratitude to him.

Thanks are also due Deborah Tewksbury of the Southeastern Vermont Regional Library for her cheerful help in obtaining many reference works. Senator James Jeffords' office rendered invaluable service in obtaining maps of the period from the Library of Congress.

Finally, without the encouragement and help of my wife, June, this book would not have come to fruition.

Contents

Foreword

by

CHARLES KURALT

George Butler causes me to shake my head in admiration. He can do anything — preach a sermon (that was his main occupation as a Methodist minister), build a house (he personally constructed much of the cozy farmhouse where he lives in Vermont), or play a concerto (he details in this book the beginnings of his life in music, with a patched-up violin and an unplayable cornet). He can also tell a story. If you like stories and sit down to listen to George at his kitchen table, it may be a while before you think to get up again.

He is a compact man with a chiseled, almost biblical face, a great shock of white hair, fierce and sparkling eyes, and a mighty voice that reverberates around a room. When I first met him in the spring of 1969, he was rambling over a snowy mountainside with his wife, June, collecting maple sap from his trees all day, and boiling it down into syrup late into the night. He was 25 years older than I, and I couldn't keep up with him. "Working hard is good for you!" he boomed as I sat and rested. "Keeps the lard off!" His syrup all graded out to the pale golden version known as "Fancy." That's the best. George doesn't just do things; he does them as well as they can be done.

He qualifies as a no-nonsense lover of animals; he and June have a close association with the Humane Society of the

United States and an abhorrence of trapping animals for their furs. He's a self taught engineer, too. One day, pondering the unnamed little stream that falls down a mountain near his house, George figured he could put that rushing water to use. Next thing I heard, he had built his own hydroelectric dam with parts he bought at the hardware store and found around the house. It's a small one, but large enough to supply all his own electrical needs for free, with power left over to sell to the local electric co-op.

In my occasional visits to the Butlers, George had given me hints of his background, but only as far back as Yale Divinity School. I still didn't know exactly where all his thriftiness, inventiveness, and energy were given birth. Now he's written this book about his boyhood, and now I know. He had a devout and kindly father; that helps account for George's own life's calling and his own kindliness. He had a provident and loving mother, whose traits he also absorbed and went on to share with the world. He had a great bear of a dog, almost a member of the family, a kind of surrogate brother. And he grew up in what he calls "simpler times."

I suppose they were simpler times, but I am sure they would baffle city children of today. Eggs had to be gathered from the henhouse; coal scuttles had to be filled and the fire restarted in the big kitchen stove on cold mornings; ice boxes had to be replenished in the summer and ice cream freezers had to be cranked by hand; gas lamps had to be lighted at dusk; and the steel needles of the Victrola had to be changed after each scratchy song.

Young George Butler grew up among hard working tradesmen of trades long-departed, the iceman, the milkman, the lamplighter, the organ grinder, the horsecar conductor, and the livery stable owner. Particularly vivid are his memories of family excursions on muddy roads in his father's recalcitrant "Tin Lizzie" and the inevitable automotive mishaps of the day.

But all George's childhood memories are clear—of sledding down Washington's hills in the winter, playing in the Capitol catacombs in summer, and sneaking a drink from a handy horse trough on the way to school. Armed with these memories, and with his father's meticulous diary of church and family affairs, he has written a valuable memoir of a vanished time. It's a personal history, and also a social history.

It's a good story, too. I've already said George Butler is a wonderful story-teller.

Simpler Times

Introduction

At one point, Lewis Carroll, the beloved creator of *Alice in Wonderland* and *Through the Looking Glass*, has the White Queen engage Alice in the following conversation:

> "... Let's consider your age to begin with—how old are you?"
>
> "I'm seven and a half exactly."
>
> "You needn't say 'exactly.'" the Queen remarked. "I can believe it without that. Now I'll give *you* something to believe. I'm just one hundred and one, five months and a day."
>
> "I can't believe *that*!" said Alice.
>
> "Can't you?" the Queen said in a pitying tone. "Try again: draw a long breath, and shut your eyes."
>
> Alice laughed. "There's no use trying," she said: "one *can't* believe impossible things."

Similarly, for a person brought up in a major American city in the first decades of this century, life in today's cities is unimaginable. My family lived in the nation's capital—my city—Washington, D.C., at the turn of the century. In this book, I have attempted to portray the urban life of that wondrous period in our history.

Today's Washington, however, is as unreal to me as the fantasy that Alice faced. Likewise, I would imagine that "my city" may seem just as fanciful to those who live in the cities of today. These stories, however improbable they may seem to many, are all true. Cities in the first decade of this century were far different from their modern metamorphoses. In many respects they were the core of the growth of America's future greatness.

"My city" was truly a city of simpler times, where progress and innocence thrived together, and where the quality of life soared. By contrast, consider today's cities, drowning in smog and congestion from millions of automobiles, where crime and drugs often combine to make the streets unsafe for all except a well-armed police force, and where civility and kindness are all too often lost in the noise and pace of modern life. In those simpler times when the auto began to replace the *clop, clop, clop* of horses with the *putt, putt, putt* of the internal combustion engine, it was a sound of liberation and freedom. Thousands of city-dwellers could now visit the surrounding countryside and travel around the city with greater speed and convenience. Crime in those long-gone times was likewise far rarer and simpler—broken streetlamps, stolen bicycles, and the like. Also, in those bygone years, the seemingly breakneck pace of life in the city was still slow enough for people to know merchants, tradesmen, and neighbors personally. Basic civility and friendliness were normal parts of everyone's life.

The tales I have included of life in these simpler times were normal occurrences. These stories of daily life took place in a time when life was every bit as friendly, open, and intoxicating as I have attempted to portray. It was an amazing period in the growth of mankind, a time of great changes and seemingly endless progress, where no problem was too great to be solved with work and determination. Electricity, telephones, automobiles, radio, refrigeration, and all the many conveniences of modern life, now taken for granted, were in their infancy, and the future seemed to hold no limits.

Values from the previous generation remained strong throughout those times, and the family unit was the basic block of American society. The city was seen as the crown jewel in the development of a society, where education, technology, and intellectual thought flourished. The church and religion played an active, daily role in the life of the city as well, providing a community of common interest, moral guidance, assistance for the poor and sick, and an uplifting belief in God and man.

These simpler times, however, should not be confused with "perfect times." Many societal problems were ignored, condoned, or encouraged. Race, the role of women, and the treatment of workers stand out among the many imperfections. Yet, this was a period of great change and growth in both the technological and philosophical nature of society. The great social changes of the later 20th century all had their roots in this amazing period in our history.

It was my good fortune to be an eyewitness to many of the wondrous developments of the 20th century, and I cannot help but look to the future of mankind with hope and envy when I review the changes of this century that have passed before my eyes. Emboldened by this knowledge; armed with my father's personal diaries, containing over half a century of family folklore and stories of city life; and reinforced with the memories of my own life, I have undertaken to write this unique tale of growing up during one of Americas most fascinating and formative periods.

CHAPTER ONE

A Cock Crows on Capitol Hill

*A*s the first rays of morning light reached the eastern-most corner of my bed, our rooster began his loud and shattering crowing, waking my family and not a few of our neighbors. You would hardly expect such bucolic sounds in the center of a major city, let alone within easy earshot of the nation's Capitol. This, however, didn't happen today; it happened in the past—just after the turn of the century at my parents' home only a block from the Capitol building in Washington, D.C.

None of our friends and neighbors kept chickens, but we did. We kept them because we had the room and because my family was frugal. Dad was an impecunious clergyman and mother's Germanic heritage bespoke thriftiness, or as she said so often, she was a *sparsam* housewife. Chickens ate table scraps supplemented with a little grain and, in exchange, provided the family with fresh eggs and excellent Sunday dinners. A fine example of early recycling.

By the time I was a toddler, the Butler "minifarm" was well established. The chickens were an institution. Occasionally, they tried their wings by flying over the high board fence. When we retrieved the errant birds, the miscreants suffered the indignity of having the feathers of one wing clipped, severely limiting their flight. Keeping chickens also taught Sis and me about chicken culture. Hens often became broody, but we learned that by dunking the broody hen in a pail of water, she would usually be cured of her desire for mother-hood. We also learned just how mad a wet hen could get.

When hens stopped laying, it was off with their heads. I don't know how Dad did it, for he was the gentlest of men. Yet, he dispatched them skillfully, and we accepted the chicken's fate as part of the eternal order of life.

As time went on and years passed, keeping chickens turned out not to be entirely fun, especially when I was put to work cleaning out the hen house. Chicken manure has an extremely pungent aroma, and ridding the hen house of this stinking mess was as miserable a job as any small boy could have. Chicken excrement is, however, excellent fertilizer, and dad made first-rate use of it. More early recycling. I hated this chore, and because I did, I dawdled, as only a young boy can dawdle, and usually ended up taking twice as long to fin-ish as necessary. My standard routine was taking a deep breath, holding my breath, and running inside for a minute of work, followed by running outside for a breath of fresh air for the second minute. At the time, I didn't know that chickens were coprophagous. Had I known it, I would have delighted in encouraging them to consume more of their own droppings, saving me the weekly task of cleaning the hen house.

Mother's father was a blacksmith at the Washington Navy Yard and in the 1880's moved to a new row house in Campbell's development at 229 Second Street, S.E. The family legend was that John Phillip Sousa, the renowned "March King" and at that time leader of the Marine Band, had planned to buy the house. Mother's parents however, working directly with Mr. Campbell rather than an agent, were able to close the deal first, saving Mr. Campbell the commission. In 1903, two years before marrying Father, Mother had, through 16 years of saving from her meager $600 a year salary as a schoolteacher, bought the house next door, number 231. It was her "investment." According to her upbringing, real estate was preferable to stocks and bonds.

Campbell had built half a dozen such row houses on Second Street, just south of Carroll Street, which was but one block long. In back of our house, spreading out behind 229 and 231, was a large inside lot on which Campbell had planned to put alley dwellings for blacks, a common custom in those days. Changes in zoning laws and municipal regulations thwarted Campbell's plans, however, and my family was able to buy this lot as well. This gave my father his "minifarm" almost next door to the Capitol. "The lot," as we called it, was surrounded by a board fence eight feet high. Our hen house stood at the end of "the lot" in an old contractor's shed left standing by Campbell's builders.

Keeping chickens in the city presented problems not faced by country folk. Even in the early 20th century, neighbors in the city objected to being awakened at the crack of dawn by a rooster's roisterous roup. Such a reveille might have been all right in the country where it was an accepted part of farm life, but in a "modern" city, people took exception. Periodically, a policeman would knock on our door. Dad would greet him pleasantly, but the officer's message was invariably grim, "Get rid of that rooster! If you don't, you'll be guilty of harboring a public nuisance." Dad, of course, always the gentleman, who had long lived by the precept, "A soft answer turneth away wrath," would respond, "I'm sorry the neighbors have been incommoded by my rooster. I'll take care of it at once."

The accepted method of dispatching a chicken was to wring its neck. Dad, however, couldn't do that. He was much too humane and tenderhearted. Holding the offending rooster by its feet, Dad would lay it on a chopping block and administer the coup de grace with one clean blow of his axe. As all little boys, I was fascinated by the reflex actions after the execution as the bird flopped around headless for several minutes.

Our large backyard lot had started out as a rather barren clay bank, but by diligent work and with the help of an endless supply of chicken manure, Dad had been able to transform it into an oasis in the middle of the city, replete with fruit trees, flowers, vegetables, and of course chickens. He had apples, Seckel and Bartlett pears, peaches, and damson plums. Dad loved flowers, and we had all kinds, especially roses, tulips, dahlias, and jonquils. A walkway down the middle of the lot had a grape arbor overhead. After the *Titanic* sank in 1912, Dad bought Concord grape vines from the surviving seamen who, having had enough of the perils of the great deep, turned to selling door to door. Dad said that these men wanted to be on "terra firma," or "terra-cotta," as he often said in jest.

We thought of "the lot" as large, but compared to what Dad wanted to do, it often seemed too small. In addition to the fruit trees, flowers, and grapes, we had lettuce, carrots, corn, beets, beans, a few heads of cabbage, and, of course, the ever-present chickens. He maintained the entire garden with hand tools and a small cultivator for which he supplied the motive power. I, of course, was recruited to weed the garden in the spots that the cultivator couldn't go, and also to clean the hen house of the ever-present chicken manure.

In Dad's diary he often referred to boarding the Old Dominion Interurban at the Virginia end of the Aqueduct Bridge, long since replaced by Key Bridge, and traveling out to visit his friend and part-time poultry supplier, Professor Kirby, at Balston, Virginia. One diary entry reads: "With Professor Kirby . . . got five chickens. One rooster weighed 9 and 1/4 pounds, four hens, $0.75 each, costing a total of $3.75. Weight in all, about 20 pounds." His mission accomplished, he then returned home aboard public transportation with his very live and loud cargo.

I was born in 1909 in Washington, D.C., at the old Providence Hospital. My father carefully recorded the events leading up to my advent into the world. His diary for May 30-31 1909, reads, "Rainy all forenoon (the 30th). About 1:30 A.M. (the 31st) Helena and I went to Providence Hospital, walking. About 8:40 P.M. our little son was born. Mother suffered greatly, though with no other injury. Child was born naturally, without use of instruments. Dr. D. Olin Leach was in charge."

Providence Hospital was two and a half blocks below our house, taking up the whole block between Second and Third Streets, and D and E Streets. It was a nondescript conglomeration of rambling, stuccoed buildings with red-tiled roofs. It sat on a slight elevation to the south of Folger Square. Stone retaining walls, several feet high, ran along Second and Third Streets as well as on the D Street side, where the main entrance was located.

Dr. Leach was our beloved family physician who took care of the entire family's medical needs. When I was born, obstetricians were relatively few, and I have no way of knowing what, if any, prenatal care Mother received. Dr. Leach, however, was present at my birth. Mother was a healthy woman who had married late in life. She had my sister two years after marrying, and I was born two years later when mother was 40. That she suffered terribly is understandable: I weighed ten-and-a-half pounds at birth. Although she endured a difficult labor, she was well aware of those around her. She even fussed at a young intern assisting Dr. Leach because he reeked of cigarettes.

As I look back at Dad's chronicle of my birth, one line stands out, "... went to Providence Hospital, walking." In 1909, nothing could have been more logical than walking down Second Street on Capitol Hill in the nation's capital in the dead of night to get to the hospital. Mother had awakened Dad late at night when she felt the beginnings of labor pains. They didn't own an automobile, nor did any of the neighbors. There was no horse and carriage readily available, and by the time Dad had awakened the stablemen at Zurhorst's livery stable several blocks away, the carriage readied and brought around, and Mother transported to the hospital, I might well have been born at home. It was far simpler and quicker to walk the few blocks to hospital.

Dad, of course, visited Mother every day in the hospital. He brought his precocious little 24-month old daughter, my sister Margaret, with him. She had begun talking before her first birthday, but she hadn't learned to walk until after our cousin, Jack, who was the same age. Margaret, however, quickly compensated for this shortcoming by declaring: "Jack can walk, but I can talk." Mother saved cookies from her daily lunch for Margaret, and told her that they came from her new little brother—a far-sighted plan to forestall sibling rivalry. Shortly thereafter, my clever sister learned a poem:

> *"Into our house one day,*
> *A dear little angel came.*
> *'Little Angel, what is your name?'*
> *He said not a word in answer,*
> *But smiled a most beautiful smile . . .*
> *My little brother . . ."*

Mothers were confined to the hospital for two weeks in those days. Fortunately, the original receipts for Mother's stay were carefully preserved in the family archives, which showed the entire hospital charges for the two-week stay to be an astounding $40. Dr. Leach, the son of a Methodist minister, mindful of the straitened circumstances of ministers, never presented a bill for his services.

Our home on Second Street was the usual, seemingly narrow-chested, three-story red brick house so common in the early days of this century. There were two front entrances, one

➤➤PROVIDENCE HOSPITAL.◄◄

———•———

Washington, D.C., May 31 , 190 9

Received of Mrs H. Butler $ 20.⁴⁵

Sister Bachman
Sister in Charge.

May 30 – June 4

➤➤PROVIDENCE HOSPITAL.◄◄

———•———

Washington, D.C., June 9 , 1909

Received of Mrs H. Butler $ 20.⁴⁵ w.

Sister Bachman
Sister in Charge.

June 7 – 13

The rather reasonable price of childbirth—1909.

leading up to the formal entrance on the second floor, and the other to the basement or first floor as we called it. The first floor was sunk just below street level. The main room, the dining room, had varnished, wainscoted walls and was lit by a Tiffany chandelier with an inverted Welsbach gas mantle. The chandelier hung over the dining room table, which often was opened to its full length to seat the many dinner guests. In the front of the room was a bay window where an old-fashioned, treadle-powered Singer sewing machine stood. The grassy front yard extended no more than ten feet from the house to the iron picket fence bordering the sidewalk.

The kitchen, the heart of the house and my favorite room, with its polished black cast-iron range was behind the dining room. A room, intended as a servant's quarters, half the width of the house, was at the back of the kitchen. We had no servants, so this became the storeroom. In the winter, a pierced tin pie safe served as the icebox. A short hall off the storeroom led to an old-fashioned water closet, which had a standard toilet seat fastened to a bench similar to one in an outhouse. The running water for the toilet was turned on by a valve to the side. A hallway ran along the south side of the house from the front to the kitchen in back. The stairway upstairs was opposite the dining room entrance.

Upstairs on the second floor where callers arrived, there was a gray oak settle conveniently placed just inside the door. This settle was a benchlike seat with arms and a chest underneath. Above and behind it were hooks for visitors' coats. Opposite the settle were stairs to the third floor. The front parlor door opened off the entrance hall. The back parlor was separated from the front by two wooden sliding doors. When open, the two parlors made one large room for entertaining. Closed, as they were most of the time, they allowed Grandma to use the back parlor as a sitting room, while the front parlor was available for unexpected guests or other family use. Grandma's bedroom was behind the back parlor. In addition to the sliding doors, access to all rooms on the second floor, as on the first floor, was provided by a hall running the length of the south side.

The top floor had four rooms plus the only full bathroom. Dad had his study in the front room. Sis had the front hall room next to the study. My parents' room was behind the study, with my small room at the back of the house next to the bathroom.

Father was a Lutheran minister. He was a slightly built man, a little below medium height, mild-mannered, every inch a gentleman. He bespoke gentility and good breeding. He wouldn't even think of appearing in public without a suit, though he never wore a clerical collar or a robe. He was down to earth with no sham or pretense. He was truly a sincere, humble Christian gentleman of the early 20th century. In my earliest recollections, Dad wore a beard, but one Sunday, an irrepressible young boy in Sunday School changed that with two short sentences. When Dad asked, "What kind of man was Saul?" The boy jumped up with the answer, " He was a rough looking man. He wore a beard!" With that one line of prejudice, Dad's beard was doomed.

Mother was rather short and had a slightly heavier build than Dad. She was, however, at all times the epitome of the late-Victorian lady, well-corseted, with chestnut-brown hair worn in a tight bun atop her head—an image that befitted her role as a quondam schoolteacher, who was now a preacher's wife. When Mother went out, she often wore a dyed black fox fur over her shoulders. Furs were a part of life; for women furs were considered necessary to being well-groomed. The terrible cruelty of the steel-jawed leghold trap had not yet been generally acknowledged. One member of the family, however, was quick to take offense. Bonnie, our new puppy, upon seeing the fox on Mother's shoulders replete with teeth and glassy eyes, left no doubt of her disapproval.

As a schoolteacher, Mother had tolerated no nonsense in her classroom. She expected no less from her own children, something that always seemed to be easier for my sister. Mother's experience in running an orderly and efficient classroom carried over to her housekeeping. She managed the house well with a sturdy resoluteness and frugality that befitted her Germanic roots.

Her mother, "Grandma Johnson," had crossed the Atlantic in 1851 aboard a sailing vessel at the age of 16 years to join her two older brothers. She carried all her worldly goods in a sea chest. Upon reaching her destination, New Orleans, she was devastated to learn that both had fallen victim to the yellow fever plague then sweeping the city. Penniless, stranded in a strange land, unable to speak a word of English, alone, and utterly forlorn, she managed to obtain employment as a servant girl with an army officer's family. The family moved several times, eventually reaching Baltimore in the later 1850's, where she met and fell in love with William Johnson. Grandpa Johnson was a Methodist of high moral character who did not drink, smoke, or use profanity. He was poor and illiterate, but he worked hard. After he mastered the blacksmith trade, they moved to Washington, D.C.

It is no wonder, with such a family background, that Mother was so practical and focused. Naturally intelligent, she graduated from high school at the age of 16 and had to wait a year before being allowed to enter normal school. When she finally became a teacher, she continued to work hard and save for her future as she had learned as a child.

Dad, on the other hand, was more the dreamer—the kindly, trusting, generous-to-a-fault preacher. If being a true Christian is not impractical, he was not actually impractical, but more "otherworldly" when compared to Mother. Dad's father had been an illustrious clergyman in Washington, D.C. and he descended from a long line of clergy. Dad's genes, inherited from his father, made him what he was. The earliest of the Butler clergy line began right after the Revolutionary War, when John George Butler, formerly of the 6th

Pennsylvania Regiment during the war, decided to study theology and became licensed to preach in the ministerium of Pennsylvania. Later he moved to Virginia and eastern Tennessee, where he established churches along the "western frontier." In 1805 he "settled" in Cumberland, Maryland, with an eight point circuit. One church was 47 miles away, and another 60 miles. His munificent salary from all eight churches was $*150* annually.

His grandson, John George Butler III, my grandfather, also entered the clergy and in 1849 became the young pastor of St. Paul's English Lutheran Church in Washington, D.C. As a young pastor, my grandfather became a commanding figure in the nation's capital. When the Civil War broke out, he declared himself foursquare for Lincoln and the Union. Some parishioners were offended and left. Others, such as the Speaker of the House and later to be Vice President, Schuyler Colfax, came and more than filled the empty pews left by the departing southern sympathizers. Lincoln appointed my grandfather one of his first hospital chaplains. Later he served as chaplain to the Fifth Pennsylvania Regiment. After Lincoln's assassination, he was appointed spiritual counselor to John Atzerodt, one of the Lincoln conspirators, and indeed walked with him to the gallows on the grounds of the old Arsenal. Shortly thereafter, he was elected Chaplain of the U.S. House of Representatives during the 41st, 42nd, and 43rd Congresses. During the 1880's, he was elected Chaplain of the Senate. All this work was only a spare-time occupation, as he followed his primary mission of establishing Lutheran churches all over the city. He was also a member of the founding faculty of Howard University Divinity School in 1870. Dad followed closely in his father's footsteps, and joined Howard's faculty in 1890.

It is no wonder that his son, Jonathan Butler did not choose the ministry, but became a storekeeper instead. He was a deeply religious man however, and served as a Sunday School Superintendent as well as a church deacon.

Jonathan's youngest son, my grandfather, at first managed his father's branch store in Berlin, Pennsylvania, some twenty miles from Cumberland. Then he heard the call to preach, although he always looked on his storekeeping experience as a most valuable preparation for the ministry in learning to evaluate human character. Storekeeping also taught him the value and use of money, and helped him form prompt and reliable business habits. After enrolling in Gettysburg College, and then its Seminary, he came to Washington in 1849 as the young pastor of the fledgling congregation of St. Paul's English Lutheran Church.

It was into this deeply religious heritage that I was born. I didn't understand my strong religious inheritance as a child, I simply despised being a "preacher's kid," although I adored my father. St Paul's words were never truer, "When I was a child, I thought as a child, I spoke as a child [I Cor. 13:11] . . ." Dad had a love and concern, a compassion for all people, indeed for all creatures great and small that surpassed my understanding. In my earliest years, I was oblivious to Dad's calling. While Mom saw me as the apple of her eye, she seldom allowed her love to overcome her good sense. Dad, however, was made for a son like me. He was ever the gentle, loving father, with more time to be with his children than the average father of the period.

My sister, Margaret Elizabeth, was my earliest friend and at the same time, the bane of my existence. Sis was a very shy, determined, and obedient little girl, every inch the perfectionist. She had lovely blue eyes and blond hair, which she wore braided in two pigtails. Once, a teacher, of whom more will be said later, told my anxious mother during a meeting over her fractious male offspring, "Well, George isn't Margaret." That comparison, expecting me to be as studious and obedient as my sister, added to the cross I had to bear. In addition to being a "preacher's kid," I had to follow this paragon of virtue all through grade school and high school. This truly seemed unfair.

Physically, Sis and I were alike, but emotionally we were very different. She was determined to have her own way; she knew what she wanted and was persistent in obtaining it. I was more easy-going, less of a grind, and certainly less studious. My round, somewhat chubby face with a dimple on only the right cheek gave me a mischievous look that complicated my attempts to appear innocent. As one teacher told Mother, I had a lot of the "Old Nick" in me. I also inherited my father's generosity and sense of fairness. Whenever my sister and I were given ice cream or fruit to share, she always asked me to divide it, knowing that I would always give away the bigger half.

When Sis made up her mind that she wanted something, she harped on it until she got it. Living in the city, my family found it impossible to keep a pony, even with our "minifarm." Since a pony was out of the question, she decided on a collie pup. Realistic goals are important if being determined is going to work, and soon she began her chant, "I want a collie pup . . . I want a collie pup . . ." Eventually, Dad saw an ad in the *Evening Star* for a collie pup costing $2.00, and our home quickly filled with joy and excitement when the puppy arrived. Sis promptly named our puppy Bonnie Jean, but the name was entirely too cumbersome for a perpetual-motion puppy, and we quickly shortened it to Bonnie. She was a purebred collie, with a sharply pointed face, long tawny hair, and a nicely feathered tail, which was always wagging.

Bonnie quickly became a beloved part of our family. At night, Bonnie was expected to stay in her bed in the back areaway in good weather, but when the folks were away or the weather was bad, there was a never-ending contest to see who could get Bonnie to spend the night in bed with them, something of which Mother deeply disapproved. We loved our four-legged friend so much, however, that we readily brooked parental disapproval whenever the opportunity arose.

Unfortunately, our much loved Bonnie was not with us for long. One morning, when Dad went to the back door to let her

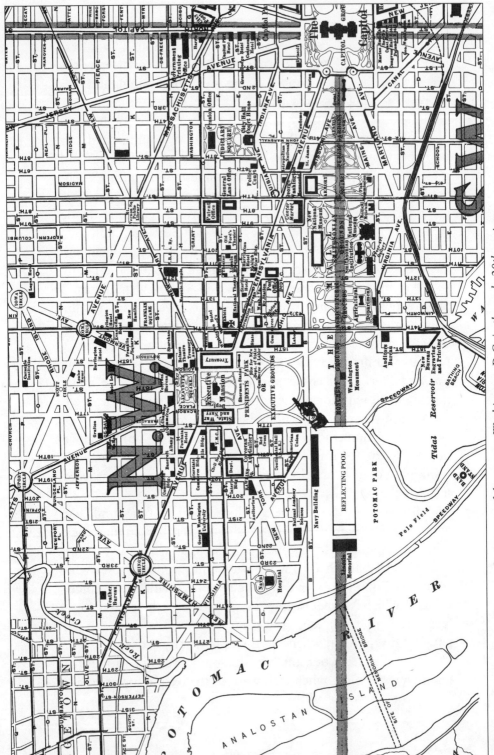

Street map of downtown Washington, D.C. in the early 20th century.

in, she didn't come. Dad found her lying behind the garage, all but dead. Somehow she had gotten into some rat poison. We were frantic. Dad brought her into the kitchen and immediately sent for the veterinarian. She lay still, her breathing shallow and rapid. Dad's diary tells the sad story beautifully: "Our dear dog Bonnie died about 10:30 this morning, the result of poisoning. We did what we could to relieve her and secured a veterinarian. But in vain. We are all grieving terribly, as though we had lost one of our best human friends. She won her place in our hearts by her love and gentleness and faithfulness."

We buried Bonnie in the backyard, and the grieving continued. "Will I see Bonnie again in heaven?" I asked Mother. "Of course dear," she replied. "When you go there, she'll be waiting to greet you." The assurance helped, but the pain continued. Time and time again as I came in from the backyard, Mother noted the sadness in my face; I was putting flowers on Bonnie's grave.

Mom and Dad knew something had to be done for Sis and me. Our neighbor, Miss Laura Buehler, had just returned from Pennsylvania with a collie and shepherd mix, which her family wanted to give away. Reluctantly, feeling somewhat like traitors, Sis and I went down to her house at Second and D Streets to see him. We were "goners" at first sight. Shep was as fat and adorable a little bundle of fur as could be found. He immediately began to entertain us by standing on his hind legs, grabbing the tablecloth in his teeth, and swinging back and forth in high glee to the mutual ecstasy of all present.

Then and there we brought Shep home, never dreaming that this cuddly little ball of fur would grow up to be a massive hundred-pound-plus dog. Our enormous Shep, an overgrown, boisterous puppy made our family wondrously happy. Shep thought the world was for playing and that chickens made great playmates. Unfortunately, he often "played" them to death. But we loved him so much, we couldn't give him away. Mother finally solved the problem by tying a dead chicken around his neck and making him wear it all day. Every time he came near us, we shamed him. As a result, he never went near another chicken, nor would he ever eat cooked chicken scraps again. His face was less pointed than Bonnie's, but he had the same handsome tawny coat. He had a white vest and limpid brown eyes that melted our hearts. Our family was complete again.

CHAPTER TWO
Gaslight Life

*T*he invention of gaslights was a great innovation and improvement over all the preceding forms of indoor and outdoor lighting, including kerosene lamps, candles, whale oil lamps, and all their assorted brethren. The gaslight age began in the United States in 1817 when the first gaslight company applied for a charter in Baltimore. Gaslights didn't arrive in Washington, D.C., for another 31 years until 1848, when the White House was "modernized" with gas chandeliers, which took the place of the existing coal oil lamps and candles.

Gaslights made their first appearance as streetlights along Washington's main streets in 1853. Gas, however, was costly, so the city fathers decreed that gas streetlights would only be on at night; they would not be lit on nights when the moon was full, whether the moon was out or not.

In 1885, Baron Carl von Welsbach, an Austrian chemist and engineer, discovered that by impregnating a fabric with a mixture of thorium and cerium oxides, a gas mantle consisting of gauze or cotton webbing would glow brightly. The Welsbach incandescent gas mantle revolutionized lighting, and soon evenings were much brighter.

We had gas jets in every room of our house, save the dining room, Dad's study, and Gramda's parlor, which had

Welsbach mantles. Candles were available if one didn't want to bother turning on the gas. They were particularly handy in going from one room to another, or in moving around the house late at night. Grandma's bedroom was on the second floor, and she always used a candle when going downstairs to the water closet late at night. It was much more practical to carry a candle with her than fuss with lighting several gas jets on her way downstairs and then turning them off on her way back.

Gas jets were small, fan-shaped hollow flanges at the end of a pipe that, when lit, spread the flame. They were located a short distance away from the wall to prevent setting the wallpaper on fire. To light one, you turned a key just under the jet, which turned on the gas. The jets emitted a small yellowish, flat flame, which dimly lit the room. They were not nearly bright enough for reading, however, and in a small, tightly closed room, the open flame could use up a shocking amount of oxygen. The Welsbach gas mantle lamps were connected to the pipes by rubber tubing. These lamps made the dim light of the regular gaslight seem even dimmer. The best light in the house was our inverted Welsbach mantle inside a Tiffany chandelier over the dining room table.

The only problem with Welsbach mantles was that they were very fragile. They were coated with paraffin to protect them in transit, but once the protective coating was melted off, prior to use, they had to be handled with great care. Even the slightest shock or careless touch could break a Welsbach mantle. If a match inadvertently touched the mantle, it could poke a hole in it and ruin it. Even a Ping-Pong ball hitting the gas chimney encasing the mantle could shatter the mantle inside.

Regardless of their fragility, these mantles provided magnificent illumination. Our first electric fixture was called a "shower" and consisted of three 25-watt carbon filament electric bulbs. When it was installed in the front parlor, we were all disappointed at the poor light given off, when compared to our Welsbach mantles.

Welsbach's work with metallic oxides was also used in fashioning early electric light bulbs. Westinghouse purchased several of Welsbach's patents and even his factory in 1906. Welsbach had also invented the first metallic filament bulb using fine osmium wires for electric lights. Osmium proved to be too costly and too rare for general use, but it paved the way for the tungsten filament of modern lights. A second application of Welsbach's work was the invention of the Aladdin kerosene lamp in 1909, which is still popular in emergencies and in the country. The Aladdin lamp gives off a strong white light and is practically smokeless and odorless.

In my boyhood, gas streetlights with Welsbach mantles were standard in Washington. The lamplighter was a familiar sight. Each evening, as dusk approached, the lamplighter made his appointed rounds. The mid-19th-century custom of not turning on streetlights when the moon was full had long since been abandoned. The lamplighter was a smallish man carrying a pole with a hook on the end and a short ladder with a curved indentation on the top step, which fitted around the fluted iron lamp post. Barely breaking stride, he would deftly hook the lever inside the globe with the prong at the end of the stick, turning up the gas so that the mantle sprang to life. Every once in a while, it would take him a little longer because the pilot light had gone out or the mantle was broken. Of this latter occurrence, we kids knew nothing! None of us would ever think about tossing pebbles at the light to break a mantle. We didn't have to think about it—we just did it, and watched with glee as the lamplighter had to climb the lamp post, take the glass bowl down, which was open-ended on the bottom, and replace the mantle. If the glass shade was cracked, he had to make another trip to replace it.

Once every month, the lamplighter came around at odd hours during the day on a cleaning trip. On these trips, he brought along a pail-full of suds, a small brush on a two-foot-long handle, and a towel stuck in his back pocket. He made his rounds quickly and professionally, accomplishing his ablutions with the extreme dexterity of long practice.

While the lamplighter took care of outside illumination, it was Dad's responsibility inside. He began the long winter evenings by taking a taper and lighting the hall gas jets. His tapers were long, thin pieces of cardboard, which he cut from scrap. This was far cheaper and convenient than lighting a match for each jet. Some families had pilot lights for their jets, but we never did. My parents considered it wasteful to have even a small flame burning constantly. Also, in the front hall, when the outside door opened, there was always the danger that a gust of wind might blow out the small pilot flame and cause leaking gas to permeate the house. One friend had flint lighters rigged to his jets so that when he pulled the string, it turned on the gas and made a spark to ignite the gas. Dad, however, felt the flint sparks were unreliable and preferred his tried and true tapers.

One of my early exploits in the gaslight age was forever seared into my memory and onto my backside. Dad was serving a mission church in the Columbia Heights section of town. Dad had started this church as a result of his father's wish and bequest. Beginning in a rented house, the church grew quickly and soon moved to a portable frame chapel. One of the time-honored traditions of raising money for a building fund was the "Oyster Supper."

Tickets were 25 cents, and the chapel was invariably full of diners. At this particular "Oyster Supper," I was a robust seven-year-old mischief-maker, surrounded by a coterie of pre-adolescent followers. The "Oyster Supper" was in full swing, and the chapel was completely filled with diners. Such portable chapels were forerunners of modular home construction. They were sold from church to church as the churches went through their growth cycle. They could be taken apart, section by section, and moved to new locations as desired. The gas line for the lights ran through the front vestibule where the gas meter and main shutoff were located. No one paid any attention to the potential for mischief that this arrangement created, but to my childish mind, this was fun just waiting to happen. Egged on by a fellow conspirator, who I was sure was highly impressed by my technical prowess, I turned off the gas main, plunging the assembly of diners into total darkness. A quick second turn, meant to turn the lights back on, managed to restore about half the mantles. The rest had cooled off, and the gas did not reignite. Everyone was in danger of being gassed, and the possibility of explosion was real. Pandemonium reigned. Men frantically searched their pockets for matches to relight the flowing jets, while several women swooned.

Dad, correctly diagnosing the difficulty, suddenly appeared in the vestibule just as I was congratulating myself on my exploit. He often quoted the scripture from Proverbs, "Foolishness is bound up in the heart of a child. The rod of correction will bring it out," and "Spare the rod and spoil the child." But he never had followed these precepts until now. He took a very dim view of my feat and, then and there, took me to the woodshed as he had never done before.

*T*hough our house was not old, it was in the Dark Ages as far as heating was concerned. We had three fires to keep going, two Latrobe stoves, and the kitchen stove, which we used in a vain attempt to keep out the cold. One of the Latrobes was in the basement dining room, and the other was in the second floor back parlor. The basement stove had registers opening off the chimney in the second floor parlor and on the third floor in Dad's study. The second floor Latrobe had only one register off its chimney in the folks' bedroom on the third floor. None of these registers produced much heat, though smoke was a different matter.

Latrobes were sometimes called Baltimore heaters because of their origin. Their inventor, John Hazelhurst Latrobe, was the son of the noted architect and engineer, Benjamin Latrobe, known primarily for his restoration of the Capitol and White House after they were burned by the British in 1812. It was Benjamin Latrobe who decided to paint over the scars and charring caused by the British on the Executive Mansion, thus giving it its name, the White House.

John Latrobe, a civil engineer from Baltimore, designed the stoves. Our Latrobes were squat and round, about 20 inches in diameter at the base; they stood about two feet high. Above the large firebox, the stove curved inward to a flattop where there was a lid for putting in chestnut-size coal. Underneath the firebox was an ash pan, which lifted out, so the ashes could be removed and unburnt pieces of coal retrieved. Just above the firebox were three isinglass, or mica, doors, through which could be seen the glowing coals. Mica was very sturdy, yet it let the heat out well into the room. These doors also allowed access to the glowing coals for lighting tapers, thus saving a match.

Emptying the ashes was far too delicate and skilled a job for one of my tender years. The fly ash would cover the room with a fine layer of dust unless extreme care were used in carrying the ash pan outside. Dad did this every morning, carefully depositing the ashes into an empty coal scuttle. The scuttle was then turned over to me and I was sent to the backyard to sift the ashes over an ash barrel. The sifter was a sheet metal box about two feet long with a hopper on one end and a hook for the coal hod to receive the unspent coals on the other. Inside was a cylinder of half-inch hardware cloth, which was turned by a hand-crank. As I turned the crank, I could make as much dust as I wanted as the pulverized ash dropped to the barrel below, and the salvageable coals clinked into the waiting scuttle behind.

In the kitchen, an old-fashioned black cast-iron range served for both heating and cooking. The range had a waterback, or water coil, on one side of the firebox that made hot water for the household. It had a 30-gallon tank and piped hot water throughout the house. The waterback did a good job when the fire was hot, but a tank of this size was soon exhausted on Saturday night when everyone took baths. Mother saw to it that we were sparing with the hot water; even so, she had to augment the supply by carrying several kettles of hot water up to the third floor from the top of the stove. To save water, Mother always bathed Sis and me together when we were very little. A real hot bath was a distinct luxury.

Most of the time, a pot of soup was simmering on the back of the stove, giving off a heavenly aroma and creating a benison foreign to modern kitchens. On cold, wet winter days, when I returned from school with my shoes and feet soaked through, Mother would take off my shoes and socks, put my feet up to dry and warm on the fender in front of the oven, and give me a cup of that wonderful soup whose magnificent aroma filled the kitchen. I probably didn't deserve such tender care because I had gotten so wet from jumping from puddle to puddle as I came home, looking for the really deep ones in which to splash around. Boys will be boys, and fortunately for boys, mothers will be mothers, loving their wayward offspring in spite of their misdeeds.

The worst part of our heating system was that all the stoves burned coal, and keeping those stoves going required bringing coal inside after dark from the coal vault. The coal vault was four feet below the basement level. It ran underneath the sidewalk to a manhole access at the curb, which allowed coal wagons to place their chutes into the manhole and dump their loads directly into our bin. While this arrangement was very ingenious, the entrance to the vault was under the iron steps to the second floor, opposite the basement entrance. It was never locked; tramps had been known to seek shelter in its depths. At night it became a dark and terrifying dungeon to me. Like all youngsters, I put off all disagreeable tasks as long as I could, regardless of the logic. The vault was dark and forbidding even in daylight, but filling those coal hods after dark was truly dreadful.

Cold winter mornings were something never forgotten. From long experience, my folks had learned that it was best to build a fire in the kitchen stove each morning, rather than trying to nurse a fire back to life from the previous evening. A fresh fire got hotter much quicker than one that had been banked for the night. While this was probably correct, it certainly didn't make the kitchen any warmer when we got up.

The inadequate heat on the third floor was especially bad on cold mornings. It was torture to have to get out of bed and step on the icy floors. Dad had an old circular coal oil stove that he kept beside the desk in his study. On cold winter mornings, he would bring it into his bedroom and turn the wick to its highest setting to provide some heat while we dressed. The stove was about 30 inches high and perhaps 12 inches in diameter. The oil reservoir, holding about a gallon, was in the bottom. If the wick wasn't clean or if it was set wrong, it emitted a memorably noxious odor, but at least we had some heat.

While we managed to survive with these primitive heating appliances, the problem of keeping foods fresh and properly cooled during Washington's notoriously hot and humid summers was another matter. Everyone had an icebox. Our iceman, Mr. Hayes, was from the Ferris Coal and Ice Company on B Street near 7th Street, N.E. He was a barrel-chested, ruddy-faced man whose gruff appearance belied his kind heart. Whenever we heard the clop-clop of the ice wagon horses coming up the street, all the neighborhood children flocked to the rear of the wagon to pick up slivers of the cooling ice and suck on them while Mr. Hayes cut the blocks to size. The iceman then used a pair of giant tongs, akin to mammoth pliers with sharp pointed ends, to carry the ice into the houses. Housewives would indicate the size of the ice they wanted by placing cards in their windows. A 15-cent block would usually last two days if we didn't open the icebox door too frequently. On special days, when Mother made ice cream, 35 cents would buy a huge 100-pound cake of ice.

My contribution for big dinners was one that I didn't mind too much—churning the ice cream. We had a gallon White Mountain freezer, which required 10 to 15 minutes of churning, depending on how cold the mixture was and the amount of ice cream rock salt used. Mother's homemade vanilla ice cream was legendary. For several days before the event, she would save the top milk from the quarts of milk delivered every morning. There was no such thing as homogenized milk. Just before the big day, she would order a quart of heavy cream. Then she would cook her mixture of top milk, four eggs, sugar, and corn starch. After this custard-like mixture cooled, she added the heavy cream and vanilla. Then my work began.

I crushed the ice in a wooden box with an axe, put the ice and salt in the tub around the can containing the mixture, and started cranking. The old White Mountain freezer was triple action. The can rotated one way, the inside of the dasher doing the same, while the outside of the dasher scraped the sides of the can going the other way. Once started I couldn't stop, else the cream would freeze to the sides of the can and it would become impossible to crank. The best part of the operation came when the ice cream was finally frozen. Mother would carefully wipe the top of the can, then open the lid and take out the dasher. That was my reward—I could lick the dasher. "Aw come on Ma," I'd say, "leave a little more on the dasher for me." Obligingly she would.

The only trouble with making ice cream for company dinners was that it was too good. Everyone wanted seconds, and rarely was there any left for the next day. If there was any ice cream left over, we could keep it over for a day.

One of my least favorite jobs was emptying the icebox drip pan. Somehow, the water never seemed clean, and I studiously avoided contact with it. The awkward-sized pan had to be emptied at least daily, lest the water from the melted ice run all over the floor.

During winter, we had no need for an icebox. The unheated storeroom off the kitchen served as our refrigerator. It was below ground level and almost always colder than outside. Try as we would, mice always seemed to get into the house, so we used the old tin pie safe. This protected foods from the mice, but the pie safe was not child proof. Sis and I loved to sneak in and pick at a turkey or chicken carcass. Such tidbits always seemed to taste so much better because of their purloined status. Our indulgent and usually well-organized mother, however, seemed oblivious to such peculations.

*F*amilies, like armies, march on their stomachs, and ours was no exception. Families in the gaslight age marched to the corner grocery store for the majority of their provisions. Aunt Margaret patronized Kyler's Market on the corner of Third and C Streets. We patronized the infant Great Atlantic and Pacific Tea Company chain store on the corner of Second and B Streets, and the smaller chain, Sanitary Grocery Company's store, on Second and C Streets. Kyler's offered more personal service and free delivery, but Mother, ever the *Sparsam* housewife, preferred saving the few cents offered by the chains' buying power.

All of these stores were typical of the period. They were operated by one man, who waited on one customer at a time. When there were no customers, the clerk busied himself stacking the shelves that lined the walls up to the ceiling. When customers arrived, the white-aproned manager/clerk stood behind the counter to wait on them. There was no self-service. The clerk used a long "grab stick" to take cans off the shelves too high to reach by hand.

After the clerk had collected a customer's order, he would quickly tote up the bill with his pencil, writing the figures on a paper "poke" or sack. None of the stores used adding machines, and Mother being a "math shark" from her school teaching days, would often catch adding mistakes. Carefully placing the order in a sack and putting the money in the till, the clerk would then turn to the next customer and begin assembling that order.

The stores were closed between noon and 1 o'clock while the one-man staff went "out to lunch." Stores had no electricity or mechanical refrigeration; they really didn't need any, as they didn't carry fresh vegetables or meat. For the most part, they carried only canned goods and staples, such as potatoes, rice, beans, and flour. They did, however, have an old fashioned icebox in which they kept perishables such as milk and butter. They also sold bread. The unwrapped and unsliced bread sold by the corner markets was delivered fresh each morning. The bakery wagon arrived early in the morning before the city was stirring. The day's supply of bread was dumped into bins outside the front door. These boxes had hinged lids to keep the weather and neighborhood animals out. They were less successful at keeping out the neighborhood children, who felt that the empty boxes at day's end made excellent hiding places. Fortunately, our neighborhood must have been composed of only the cleanest children and the finest grade of dirt because I never heard of anyone getting sick from the bread that was dumped on top of the dirt we tracked into our favorite hiding spots. These were "sanitary markets" indeed!

While these grocery stores did sell milk, most people had their milk delivered directly to their houses by the dairy. Every day, between five A.M. and six A.M. the milk wagons made their rounds. If you awakened early or easily, you could hear the rhythmic sound of the horses hoofs as they traveled their daily routes. The horses knew the routes and stopped automatically at each house where milk was to be delivered. The milk was packaged in glass bottles with small paper stoppers. When the bottle was empty, the housewife washed out the empty bottle and put it outside for the milkman to pick up for future use. If customers wanted to change their standard orders or wanted something extra, they just left a note in the empty bottle. If the milkman had several customers in a row, he would place up to eight quarts in his metal basket, and as he went from house to house, he would call softly to his horse who would obediently keep pace with him. On cold winter mornings when the temperature took a nose dive, we would often find the lids on our milk bottles several inches above the neck by the time we arose and brought them inside.

Once a week, generally on Saturdays, Mother, Dad, and the family, including our enormous pet, Shep, would go to Eastern Market. The building took up the entire block on Seventh Street, S.E., from North Carolina Avenue to C Street. It was a long, red brick building, oblong in shape, somewhat resembling a trolley carbarn. The peaked roof was supported by cantilevered trusses with long, horizontal iron tie bars holding the two walls together.

Outside the market on Seventh Street, curbside stalls lined the block for farmers to display their fresh produce. They came from such "remote" places as Oxon Hill, Maryland, where truck farms abounded. In order to get to the market by seven A.M., these farmers got up around three A.M., loaded their wagons, hitched up their teams, and drove ten or twelve miles into the city. Once at their stalls, they unloaded their wagons, unhitched and tethered their teams, and spent the day working to sell their produce. At the end of the day, they loaded up any unsold items and began the long trek home.

Conscientious shoppers learned that it paid to arrive early if they wanted their pick of vegetables. As a little fellow, I loved those trips to the market. The smells, sounds, and sights were different from anything else, and somehow seemed exotic. As a special treat, I could usually wangle 15 cents to buy some imported Swiss cheese at Mr. Doerr's stand at the south end of the market. Swiss cheese was my favorite, probably because of

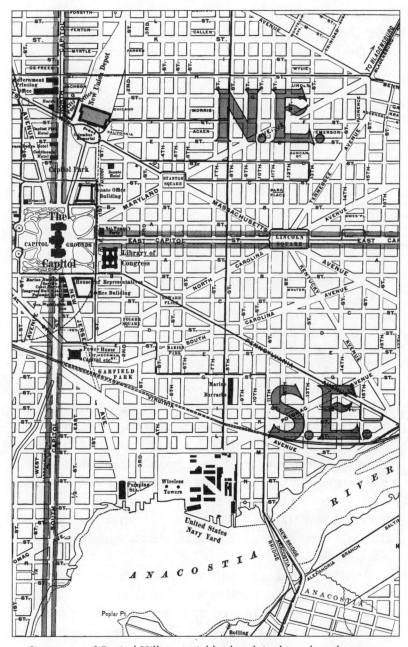

Street map of Capitol Hill, my neighborhood, in the early 20th century.

the added mystery of just how the cheesemaker put those holes in the cheese.

The north end of the market was given over, for the most part, to fruit stands. Refrigerated rail cars, relying on ice and sawdust brought all manner of oranges, bananas, and more exotic items from abroad to market. One of the fruit vendors was a short, rotund, and very jolly Italian whose produce quality was better than his English. Recently arrived in this country, he had but a limited command of English. On seeing Shep, his face always broke out in a wide smile as he exclaimed with pleasure, "Himma bigga dogga," as he patted Shep on the head.

No one thought it improper for our dog to accompany us on our tour through the market. Our butcher, Mr. Acton, went to the slaughterhouse early every day to bring back his daily meat supply. He always managed to remember to bring back an extra knuckle bone on Saturdays for Shep.

Mr. Acton displayed his meat on a long table, protected from the dust and flies stirred up by the hustle and bustle of the market by a cheesecloth. He lifted the cloth so his customers could carefully select their steaks or roasts. He was always smiling. His white apron was nearly always blood-stained from cutting and sawing the custom cuts of meat requested by his customers. He did all his cutting and trimming by hand, his razor-sharp knives silently shaping and sizing the meat. He was a real master of his trade, and I would watch in unending fascination as he worked swiftly and deftly. His technique for tying up a roast was truly a work of art. Mother knew from long experience that she could rely on Mr. Acton's judgment when it came to meat.

When I got older, my trips to the market turned even more profitable. For years, I had watched with envy as a band of juvenile entrepreneurs offered their services carrying groceries to unaccompanied lady shoppers. These boys, lined up with their little express wagons, would shout in chorus, "Baskets carried"! I couldn't wait to join their ranks, and as soon as mother let me, I became one of them. The uniformed market master, who kept order in the market, maintained a close watch on us to ensure we were well-behaved.

My goal was to develop regular customers, ladies who were satisfied with my work and would select me each week to carry their baskets. The usual fee for a block or two was 10 cents. Once in a while, when a customer lived beyond Lincoln Park, I was rewarded with a whole quarter! Earning 50 cents on Saturday morning ensured a good week and meant that I could consider myself rich.

Express wagons served a variety of uses in the age of gaslights. When a medical emergency befell me, Mother's only recourse was to load me into my little express wagon and haul me to the neighborhood physician a few blocks away. Our real family doctor, Dr. Leach, lived much further uptown, and in childhood medical crises, the hour it would take to get there was not realistic. We had no car or horse and buggy during my early years, and when my mother felt I needed immediate attention, we went to Dr. Ober on B Street across from the Library of Congress.

My first trip via express wagon occurred when I was but a toddler. I fell down the outside basement stone stairs and split my forehead open. I was bloody, bawling, and terrified. Upon arrival, Dr. Ober examined the wound, cleansed it with iodine, and sewed the skin together amid my screams of pain. Dr. Ober used no anesthetic.

A second trip came a short time later when I broke my arm. Several years after the event, my teacher gave us an assignment to write the story of our lives. The incident was so seared in memory that I made it the opening of my story. I wrote: "Almost the first thing in my life I remember is the breaking of my arm. I had hold of the iron fence around my front yard when my sister came out and said she could pull me off it. I said she couldn't. So she began to try. At first I held fast. But then she gave me a jerk and my left arm at the shoulder pulled out of its socket.

"I let go, screaming at the top of my voice. My arm hurt awful. Once more, Ma was ever ready. She hauled me around to Dr. Ober's in my wagon. He examined me carefully. 'There is no break,' he said, 'just a muscle sprain. The pain will go away in a couple of days.'

"But the pain wouldn't go away. After two days of sleepless agony, my folks finally took me uptown to George Washington University Hospital on H Street, N.W. Lying on that awful hard X-ray table with the massive tube of the X-ray over me, I was real scared. The doctors finally found that I had pulled my arm out of the socket."

Once finding the cause of my misery, the hospital doctors quickly put the arm back in its shoulder socket and the pain was relieved. Dad, chronicling this event in his diary with his usual sense of delicacy, said simply, "A little playmate broke George's arm."

The usual injuries of childhood, such as bruises and cuts from going barefoot in the summertime, were treated by Mom and Dad's favorite nostrum, "Resinol." My folks believed that this dark, tar-like, evil-smelling salve was good for what ailed one. As the "snake oil" sales pitch proclaimed, it was, "Good for bites, bunions, blisters, boils, bruises, or what have you"! If I had a sore, Dad put "Resinol" on it. If I had a cut, Dad put "Resinol" on it. Dad was a true believer, and psychosomatic or not, things felt better with "Resinol."

There were a whole group of patent remedies available to families of the period. "Fletcher's Castoria" was a staple of our medicine chest, and little wonder with a snappy advertising campaign that had billboards around the land proclaiming, "Children cry for it." Other favorites were "Sal Hepatica" and "Mrs. Winslow's Soothing Syrup." "Mrs. Winslow's Syrup" was indeed soothing; it contained a heavy dose of opium.

Other nostrums many parents used included hanging a little sac of asafetida or camphor around their child's neck. Like a religious charm, it was supposed that the noxious fumes would ward off disease. Baking soda and lime water were also popular. If a stomachache were accompanied by a headache, as it usually was for me, a hot mustard footbath was in order. Mother began by putting dry mustard in a pan of hot water. When the mixture was at full potency I was told to put my feet in the pan. This procedure theoretically drew the blood from my stomach and head to my feet, which would bring relief. If perchance the malady was an incipient cold, a mustard plaster was applied to my chest.

One advantage of being the second-born child was that my sister managed to bring home all the childhood illnesses when she started school, so I was able to have chicken pox, mumps, measles, German measles, and scarlatina before starting school. It was great comfort lying in bed, knowing that I was not missing any of my valuable school-time. Anyway, that's what Mother said. When Sis came down with diphtheria, however, medicine had progressed to the point where we were required to post a pink sign on the front door, "Quarantine! Communicable Disease." Without antibiotics, this disease brought terror to everyone, and I was shipped off to stay with my Aunt Margaret for the duration.

Our regular doctor, Dr. D. Olin Leach, was a jovial man with a great sense of humor. A family doctor in the first decades of this century was not the white-coated antiseptic, physician of today, but a family friend, concerned with all aspects of family life. He was, in a very real sense, a part of the family. Not only did he usher me into this world, but also, throughout the early part of my life, he was a wise, humane, understanding counselor and pre-eminent practitioner of the Hippocratic oath. He was mother's beau ideal. If people couldn't pay his modest charges, he never pressed them. He was a true gentleman.

One afternoon, Dr. Leach was out making house calls. After one stop, he got in his car, a deluxe model 1916 Ford Model T with oversize tires, oversize fenders, and best of all, a mechanical starter mounted at the bottom of the dashboard. When the engine was warm, one pull on this starter would invariably make the engine spring to life. This time, however, it was different. Dr. Leach turned on the ignition and gave the starter a tug. Nothing happened. He tried again. Nothing happened again. After several more fruitless attempts, Dr. Leach, familiar with the idiosyncrasies of the car, resignedly got out and manned the handcrank. Nothing happened. He tried again. Still nothing happened when he spun the crank. Preparing for a real battle, he removed his collar, tie , and coat. He cranked some more. The engine remained lifeless. The cantankerous contraption just refused to start. Perspiring and perplexed, the good doctor finally sat down on the curb to rest and mop the sweat from his brow. A small urchin, who had been standing silently on the sidewalk watching the proceedings intently, finally said to him, "Say Mister, why don't you cuss?" Dr. Leach laughed and turned to the little boy and said, "I don't know that it would do me any good, sonny."

"I dunno," said the little boy, "but it would sure make you feel a damned sight better!"

After Dr. Leach recovered, he got up and gave the balky crank one more turn, and *mirabile dictu*, the engine sprang to life. Turning to the urchin, Dr. Leach took out a quarter and said, "Here, sonny, you've been my mascot."

Later, in 1916, when Dr. Leach bought a new Velie, a luxury car with an electric starter, he sold my folks his deluxe Model T with the wonderful mechanical starter. After that we got a chance to learn firsthand just how fine and awful the mechanical starter could be.

When medical problems got really serious for our family, we had an ace-in-the-hole that most families didn't have. Dad's brother, Uncle Will, was an eye, ear, nose, and throat specialist at George Washington University Medical School. Dad and his brother were very close throughout their lives. Both had graduated from Columbian Preparatory School, with Uncle Will getting his M.D. degree from the Columbian School of Medicine in 1882, the same year that Dad received his M.A. from Columbian College. Columbian changed its name to George Washington University in 1904. In 1887, both Will and Dad went to Germany for further study, Dad in theology and Will in his medical specialty.

My first personal experience with Uncle Will's medical expertise was in 1916 when I had my adenoids removed. Dad noted the event in his diary on April 25, but what he failed to note is that Uncle Will, assisted by Dr. James Moser, performed the surgery in Dad's study. I was nearly seven and remember it well. Our house became the hospital, and Dad's study the operating room. Dad cleared off his flattop desk and Mom laid a clean sheet over it to serve as the operating table. We had no electricity, but more than adequate light was provided by the large bay window in front of the desk. Ether was the anesthetic of choice for operations at that time, and Dr. Moser soon put me to sleep. Uncle Will did the rest. When I awoke, my adenoids were gone, and the next day, Mother let me go out to play. Simpler times indeed!

When Dad's father died in 1909, he had left the then-magnificent bequest of $5,000 in his will to begin a mission church in the Columbia Heights section of the city. Dad determined to make his father's dream a reality and began the monumental task of starting a new congregation. He began by canvassing 1500 homes in that part of the city using his "wheel," or bicycle as we say now. One raw day in January, when he had been out calling, he was caught in a heavy storm and got soaked. He came home chilled to the bone; Mother's favorite cure, hot soup and dry clothes in front of the oven, was of little help. He became feverish and went to bed. Mother sent for Dr. Ober who very obligingly came right over. He gave Dad a quick exam and pronounced it a bad cold.

Mother, however, remained skeptical and watched over Dad carefully. Intuitively, she felt that Dad was much sicker than Dr. Ober thought. Her fears were not calmed by the doctor's assurances to the contrary. A short time later, she called Uncle Will, who came over immediately. He took one look at his brother and pronounced the dreaded word, pneumonia. Uncle Will quickly called his friend, Dr. George Acker, one of the leading physicians in the city for a consultation. Dr. Acker was a slightly built man in his mid-fifties, who looked every inch the classical physician of the day—pince-nez glasses, impeccable dress, and a glass-enclosed, silent, electric runabout with a tiller for a steering wheel. He looked Dad over, listened to his lungs, checked his temperature, and confirmed Uncle Will's diagnosis.

Dad was in bed for 12 weeks, requiring round-the-clock care, and was near death on several occasions. It was during this period that Buffy, our favorite chicken, saved the day.

Sis and I had names for most of our chickens, but Buffy was special from the beginning. She was as beautiful a little chick as we had ever seen. She was a perfectly adorable, reddish-brown, fluff ball who earned her name on first sight. She seemed to be a part of the family from the beginning, and was always around when we were working in the garden, usually earning herself a bonus of fresh worms.

When Dad was at his sickest, all the other hens had stopped laying for the winter, but not Buffy. All through Dad's ordeal, Buffy contributed her welcome eggs to help him get well. They were often the only food he could eat, and they provided the nutrition and sustenance that allowed Dad to overcome pneumonia.

When Dad was on his feet again, he rewarded Buffy by going over to Anacostia ". . . to obtain some Rhode Island Red eggs, so that Buffy could sit on them." Buffy may not have known she was a heroine, but a grateful family remembered her "eggsemplary" performance. She remained a part of our family circle until 1924 when she died of natural causes and went to chicken heaven.

*M*usic in gaslight America was very much a do-it-your-self activity. For those inclined toward prepackaged music, there were several options. There was no electronic music but there were mechanical gramophones or Victrolas with their huge cornucopia-shaped horns, music boxes, player pianos, and of course, every youngster's favorite, organ-grinders.

The organ-grinder man, with his pushcart organ and pet monkey, made surprisingly good music. The organ he pushed was called a hurdy-gurdy, whose design dated from the late Middle Ages. It was a stringed instrument, played by turning a crank, which in turn turned a wooden wheel causing the various strings to vibrate. Barrel organs, like hurdy-gurdies, were used for street music and activated by a similar crank. With the barrel organ, the crank operated a rotary cylinder, whose pegs opened various pipes to let in air.

Every few days, our peripatetic organ-grinder man with his pet monkey perched atop his shoulder made his appearance. Like all pushcart vendors of the age, this street musician supplied the motive power for his cart. The organ was balanced atop a light, two-wheeled cart resembling a sulky. When he moved it from place to place, he pushed the entire assemblage, walking between the shafts of the cart. Whenever he spotted a likely audience, usually a group of children, he deployed the retractable stand and began turning the crank. The concert had begun. The trained monkey leaped off his master's shoulder and started working the crowd. The monkey was clad in a gaudy red sash and a hat perched saucily on his head. He would doff the hat when a coin clinked into the bottom of his proffered tin cup.

With the monkey taking care of the financial end, the organ-grinder man grinned from ear to ear at the joyous squeals of his juvenile audience. The sounds from the organ made truly delightful and unique music. Many great composers, such as Franz Josef Hayden, had written music for these street organs, but our organ-grinder man, being Italian, always ground out *Funiculi, Funicula*. As the spirited music filled the street, more children poured out of the homes within earshot. Even housewives, enjoying a break came out, aprons and all, to participate in the festivities. As long as coins plinked into the monkey's tin cup, the music continued.

One day, for a few pennies more, the kindly Italian even let me play the organ, admonishing me as I turned the crank, "Don't stop cranking in the middle of the piece. You might ruin the organ." Cranking away with great gusto and not a little concern, I finished the piece to the delight and admiration of all my gathered friends.

Even though Thomas Edison had invented his talking machine in 1878, few people had mechanical gramophones in my early youth. Even after the machines changed from cylinders to a rigid, thick disk, the sound from these disks, while amazing, was not particularly good. The disks recorded hardly any of the bass, and the music was thin and scratchy with lots of background noise. Sometime after 1916, Uncle Will gave us his old spring-loaded Victrola, which his daughter had replaced with an electric player that used the new 78-RPM records. To make the old machine play, you had to wind the spring, place the needle on the disk, and release the drive. We had to change the needle after every disk, and if you forgot to wind the spring, the player would grind to a slow stop midway into the next tune. At first, Sis and I were fascinated with our new toy, but we soon tired of it. It just wasn't worth listening to. We would rather make our own music.

Dad was naturally musical, so musical in fact, that his father had forbidden him to take lessons out of fear that he might become a musician and join the circus. He had taught himself to play the piano, flute, and piccolo. On the other hand, Mother had had piano lessons as a young woman, but had little musical aptitude. Somewhere along the line, Dad had picked up an old high-cheeked Stainer model violin, and as soon as I could hold it, he strung it up for me and let me "saw away" on it in time as he played the piano. At that time I didn't know how to "stop" it, but I enjoyed "playing along" with him. Never mind the discords. I loved to "saw away" to the beat of "Onward Christian Soldiers," happy as a lark.

When I was seven, a representative of the Washington Academy of Music called with an alluring sales pitch. The magnificent title of the school belied the humble nature of the actual academy, a dingy, interior rented room on the second floor of a run-down building on F Street. If my parents would purchase music lessons for 50 cents a week, the academy would provide the violin. After a quick family meeting, I was enrolled in the Washington Academy of Music.

The academy's method of instruction was a second cousin to the "think system" postulated by the well-known Professor Harold Hill of *Music Man* fame. With the instructor at the head of the class, 15 to 20 youngsters were lined up and began to "saw away" in "unison." If one student blew a note, the pupil next to him was supposed to correct him. It didn't work that way. The resultant cacophony emanating from such sessions was enough to make cats howl blocks away. Somehow, in a few weeks, I was actually playing "America." My folks were very pleased with the progress, but after two years during which I learned several good things along with a lot of bad habits, they felt it was time for a change.

Reviewing my progress, my folks decided to find a new "Professor," as all music teachers were called in those days. Soon I began my lessons with a new "Professor." Unfortunately, he was an illiterate with a totalitarian approach to music. He went so far as to strap my right arm tightly to my body so I could not raise the elbow while bowing. As a result, I hated him and was beginning to hate the violin as well.

Seeing a crisis brewing, a family friend suggested a switch to Professor Joe Harrison. A bona fide musician, Professor Harrison had played with the Philadelphia Symphony and was the music director at the Ninth Street Christian Church. Under his tutelage my musical development improved dramatically and my love for music was rekindled. My progress was so good that Professor Harrison felt I needed a new violin. My old one had been seriously damaged when it fell to the ground from my bicycle, and had a bolt holding the neck together.

A pair of excellent violin makers, Strubel and Wines, were located on Fifth Street, N.E., just south of Stanton Square. Professor Harrison assured me that if I could obtain one of their violins, I would have a really fine instrument that would carry me through a lifetime. Unfortunately, such a violin cost around $150, which seemed prohibitive to all of us.

When Christmas came, I was flabbergasted. There under the tree was a beautiful new violin case. It had the latest device: a zippered velvet inside cover that would not let the instrument fall out even if the case opened accidentally. Curiously, I pulled the zipper, and behold, there was a beautiful new violin resting in its green velvet nest, protecting its finish from dust and ensuring its safety. Dad's diary explained the feat this way: "Helena and I at Professor Harrison's for a violin for George. Also at Mr. Strubel's. Engaged one for $75.00, also a fine case for $12.00, less a discount of $15.00 for my old violin."

As I fondled that beautiful violin that sparkling Christmas morning, Dad told me the story behind his find. This particular violin used to belong to an old lady who played on street corners to eke out a living. When the old lady died, her violin was consigned to her daughter's attic until one day it was found by the daughter's children, who broke it. The daughter gathered up the pieces and gave them to Mr. Strubel, who had taken care of the violin gratis for years. The back, neck, and sides were still good, but the top was ruined. Mr. Strubel patiently put the violin back together along with a new top, and made a good instrument out of it. The original parts of the violin dated back to France around 1840. They made for a very mellow and unique instrument.

As I played my new violin and reawakened it, Professor Harrison said, "You know George, your violin is much better than the ones Mr. Strubel makes entirely. It has a much stronger, mellower tone." As always, Dad had outdone himself.

CHAPTER THREE
Getting Around

*P*eople think of the bicycle as something that has been around forever. In truth, the "safety bike," as the ordinary bicycle was called at first because both wheels were of the same diameter, was invented in 1885. It replaced the high-front-wheel and small-rear-wheel bikes that had been in use for a relatively short time. These "boneshaker" bikes had come on the market in 1869. They had been invented by a Frenchman who had conceived the idea of attaching pedals directly to the hub of the front wheel. The larger the diameter of the front wheel, the farther the bike traveled with each rotation of the wheel. One complete turn of a five-foot wheel enabled the bike to travel 15.7 feet. Front wheels became bigger and bigger to enable riders to go faster and faster. Conversely, the larger the wheel, the greater the chance of a nasty fall.

"Boneshakers" had their advocates. The 1878 edition of the *Encyclopedia Brittanica* praised these bikes with the fulsome words, "With the exception of (ice) skating, bicycling is the quickest means of locomotion that man possesses . . . A fair bicyclist can outstrip a horse in a day, whilst an expert can do so in an hour. . ." To show how fast these bicycles could go over a level cinder track, the article continued, ". . . a run of 106 miles was accomplished in 7 hours, 58 minutes, and 5.5 seconds." A London newspaper, commenting on the feat, called it, "The most extraordinary performance on record of any man, animal, or machine."

Just a few years before the introduction of the "safety bike," James Dunlap, an Englishman, invented the pneumatic tire to replace the hard India-rubber tires. His invention came in the fullness of time. Pneumatic tires made bicycles far safer and more comfortable, and the chain drive of the "safety bike" made possible smaller wheels and shorter falls. It was because of these twin inventions that the bicycling craze of the "Gay 90's" took off.

As a toddler, I remember Dad's old bicycle standing forlornly in the dark basement hall of our house. At that time, I didn't understand what an important role his bike had played in his earlier life. It had been indispensable for both work and pleasure.

In his early years, Dad had used his bicycle to go to church because he liked to ride and because such transportation did not make anyone work on the Sabbath. He lived by the Biblical commandment, "Remember the Sabbath day to keep it holy . . ." He had ridden his bicycle in the same way in Reading, Pennsylvania, after his graduation from Union Theological Seminary. In Reading, he served a church as an interim pastor for a short time. Dad, however, was Washington-born, and wanted to return to his roots.

In the early 1890's, with the help of his father, he returned to Washington to start a missionary project in the northeast section of the city. Grandpa Butler was literally the patriarch of the Lutheran Church in Washington, and Dad had some big shoes to fill. Dad's mission grew from its humble beginnings in a former Chinese laundry into what was known at one time as the largest Lutheran congregation in the city. His "wheel" or bicycle was an integral part of his early work. His diary entry for February 14, 1892, illustrated the utilitarian value of his bicycle, "Cloudy and several showers today, yet rode my wheel.

There have been only two Sundays since beginning work at Keller when I could not ride."

The side of bicycling devoted to pleasure is ever present in his diaries. For instance, "August 7, 1890, A party of us went to Cabin John Bridge." Several folks, including Dad, rode their bicycles. "Took lunch along and ate it at the bridge and had a splendid time. Met Will on the return trip, several miles out, he not being able to leave earlier."

Cabin John Bridge was famous all over the world. It is a work of beauty, spanning the deep, wooded valley of Cabin John Creek, 57 feet below. It carried the Washington aqueduct over the ravine, bringing water from Great Falls on the Potomac to the city. For its first 40 years, Cabin John Bridge was the longest single-span masonry bridge in the world. It was completed in 1863 by Captain Montgomery C. Meigs. Several years after the bridge was finished, brownstone balustrades were added when it was decided that the bridge would also have to carry vehicular traffic. These stone parapets have a jog in them a few feet out from each end. One oft-repeated story in my childhood circle of confidants, told of a daring bicycle rider who successfully rode his bicycle across these stone parapets, somehow negotiating the jog, successfully defying the danger of a fall into the yawning canyon below.

In Dad's days, at the end of the 19th century, bicycling was great fun. There were no autos to scare the "liverlights" out of cyclists, and save for the occasional horse, wheelmen had the road to themselves. The joys and travails of biking are graphically depicted in the following entry in Dad's diary for April 13, 1891, "Mr. Luther Derrick and I started on our wheels for Glen Echo, then a Chautauqua, just a short distance below Cabin John [Chautauquas were a secular and religious educational movement similar to the Lyceum.]. On arriving there we decided to go on to Great Falls. The road was in excellent condition, except about two miles from the end where it was muddy and hilly. On returning, we came down the still ruined canal which was without exception the worst place I've ever been with a bicycle. Had to pick it up and carry it at a number of places. On return home found some arbutus." The "canal" was, of course, the Chesapeake and Ohio Canal, paralleling the Potomac River and running from Georgetown to Cumberland, Maryland. Though the C&O Canal was originally planned to go all the way to the Ohio "Wilderness," the age of the railroad cut short the canal era, and it was never finished.

On another occasion, Dad cycled out to the then "under construction" National Zoological Garden, which was located to the east of Connecticut Avenue, spanning the valley of Rock Creek Park. His diary entry for September 21, 1891, reads in part, "I visited for the first time the Zoological Park on the Davis' farm. Things are by no means fixed up yet, but work is progressing." Just after visiting the zoo, he proudly relates, "Bought a Victor bicycle today. Been used some before. Paying $120. Had looked at Psycho, Columbia, Premier, and Rambler." Considering the cost of this bicycle, compared to his paltry salary of less than $40.00 a month as a missionary pastor, this was an enormous investment—for a second-hand bike at that.

Apparently it was worth it. He writes immediately after his purchase, "At night, rode to Takoma, with . . . Ellie [his sister] and Will. Glorious ." Takoma was a reference to Takoma Park, a small suburban village half in the District of Columbia and half in Maryland.

When repairs to his bicycle were needed, Dad's diary records that business ethics in the bicycle trade were exceptional, at least at top-quality shops. His entry demonstrates the integrity of the period, "Saturday my wheel broke, and today I got it from the shop [Victor]. They put in a whole new frame and didn't charge a thing."

Dad soon joined the League of American Wheelmen. This organization had been formed in 1880 and was a leader in the crusade for better roads. On Memorial Day, 1892, at a band concert in Lafayette Square, Dad's diary records that he, "Presented my name to Philo Bush for membership in the League of American Wheelmen. I had been thinking about it for some time, and he wanted to get up a club of names."

Dad took his membership in the league seriously. Within a month, he noted, "Trip to Watkins Glen, Niagara, and Toronto. Convention of the League of American Wheelmen. Went by train to the Glen." He then biked the rest of the way. His diary also noted, "The wheels were carried free by the railroad." Somehow Dad's membership card has been preserved; he was member number 40066. The membership data on the back of the card explained:

> "The membership represented by this ticket expires in one year. To renew it, send your name and number and one dollar to the secretary at any time between April 1, and June 30, next year.
> "Write your autograph on the blank space below in order that hotel and club men may identify you as the one whose name is on the face of the ticket.
> "In case the ticket is lost, the loss must be certified to the secretary before a new ticket can be issued. Torn or defaced tickets can be replaced at any time. In every case, ten cents will be charged for a new ticket.
> "This ticket must be shown in order to obtain special hotel rates or other special privileges. Loaning this ticket will lead to the expulsion of the member.
>
> Albert Bassett, Secretary"

My first bicycle was not really a bicycle, but a velocipede or tricycle. By the time I was eight, however, nothing could satisfy me except a real bicycle. My friend, "Bones," had one, and he wasn't any older than I was. Every chance I got, I sneaked around to his house and, for five cents, he'd let me ride from Second Street down to the corner of First Street and back. What a businessman he was! Soon I ran out of nickels, and "Bones" had a pocketful. "Bones," however, being basically a charitable

Membership in the powerful League of American Wheelmen was a great investment in 1894.

sort, said he'd ride me on the bar of his bike. He had seen others do it. Ergo, he could do it too. We started off, and after a few unsteady turns, he lost complete control, and I fell off backwards and landed on my head. I came to on the basement steps of a neighbor who was splashing cold water on my face. Somehow I made it home and decided to acknowledge a headache, but, in homage to the code of youthful male silence, I did not discuss my backwards trip off the bar of "Bones'" bicycle. Mother was immediately concerned and reminded me that I was to be in a church play later that evening. Gently, she put me to bed and let me sleep until dinner. At mealtime, I still had a headache, and Mom determined that I needed my first-ever aspirin. Thoroughly medicated and still carrying the secret of my accident, I somehow managed to go to church and take part in the play. Fortunately, youth has been given amazing recuperative powers. This tends to counterbalance the lack of experience.

In 1917, my folks saw an advertisement in *The Evening Star* for a second-hand Hudson bike. It didn't have fenders or mudguards, and its tires were old and porous, but the Hudson did have a "New Departure Coaster Brake." The bike cost $18, and the necessary tubes of Neverleak Tire Fluid cost 25 cents each. The price seemed high, but we were suffering wartime inflation. I had saved up a good part of the cost by carrying baskets at the Eastern Market, and as usual, my beloved Mom and Dad made up the difference. I had my heart's desire, an honest-to-goodness *two-wheel bike*. The first thing I had to do was pass "the acid test." I had to pedal the bike all the way up Capitol Hill without getting off. Somehow I did—I was a bona fide bike owner.

My joy, however, was short-lived. I often left my bike in the front yard during the day, just inside the iron picket fence. The alternative was to "put it away," something no typical youngster ever did without resistance. In my defense, "putting it away" meant lugging the bike down the basement steps and placing it in the front hall, where it was never available when I needed it in a hurry. Surely, no one would steal it since he would have to come through the gate and across the front lawn to get it. But someone did, and I never saw that bike again.

The next Christmas, however, Santa Claus, knowing my yearnings, replaced the stolen Hudson with a brand new Aviator from Hiam's Bike Shop on the corner of First and B Streets, S.E., across from the House Office Building and the Library of Congress. I was very proud of my new bike. It cost $45.00 and had mudguards with gaudily painted red striping. There was, however, one fly in the ointment: Sis wanted to ride, and since the family couldn't afford two bikes, it was decreed that I should teach Margaret how to ride.

A few mornings later, I reluctantly said, "C'mon," and Sis and I went out front. I held the bike steady while she clambered aboard. We started our trip down Second Street very slowly and tipsily. Pretty soon, she was able to keep herself upright as she gathered speed and I let go. Sis was riding by herself as I ran alongside. She was also scared to death. The bike slowly began to pick up speed as it rolled down the slight incline on Second Street, and soon I couldn't keep up with her. I sat down on the curb and yelled at her from my vantage point, "Keep it up, You're doing fine!" She couldn't hear me, however, as she was screaming at the top of her voice. She wanted off, but the bike kept picking up speed. Her pigtails were flying, her arms rigid, her eyes stark with terror. Her face was contorted with fear and horror as the bike kept accelerating. By the time she came to the end of the block at D Street, she was really moving.

In my youthful exuberance of getting her upright and "being in charge," I had neglected to tell her how to use the coaster brake. Somehow she managed to turn the corner at D Street before disaster struck. Unable to stop herself and seeing that D Street was steeper than Second, she headed straight for a tree box, bringing the bike to an immediate stop. She landed in a heap at the foot of the tree, madder than the broody wet hens we had dunked so often. She was bruised and scratched, but no bones were broken. Her opinion of her brother was unprintable, and when Mom heard her tale, she took a most uncharitable, and in my humble opinion, unfair view of my endeavors. No bike-riding for me for a week, all because I tried to help.

*M*arine sharks are not known to inhabit the Potomac River. There are others, of course. Human varieties abound, such as loan sharks, confidence men, swindlers, some politicians, and those who prey on the gullible and elderly folk everywhere. Yet 100 years ago, there was a different variety of "shark" running up and down Washington's main thoroughfares to the delight and amusement of mischief-makers, both young and old, and to the consternation of the authorities.

As cities and populations grew at the beginning of the 20th century, the problem of getting around began to outpace all others. The earliest solutions for public transportation were horsecars, which were rail lines with wooden passenger cars pulled along the tracks by horses. As I was growing up, old-timers told endless stories of bygone horsecar days. Most had their roots in fact, though the incidents had the amazing ability to occur in different cities depending on where the story was being told. One early favorite was about a horsecar driver who taught his mule to chew tobacco. One day, the driver stopped at a tobacco shop to buy a quid. The mule's sense of smell combined with his addiction to the filthy weed and his innate stubbornness led to the driver's undoing. As the driver was about to pay for his purchase, the anxious animal, following one of his favorite scents, pulled the car off the track and crashed through the store window into the tobacconist's shop. Another favorite was about the farmer who bought several old horsecar mules for his farm. He soon found that they could pull the cultivator uphill just fine, but upon reaching the top, they would try to jump on the cultivator and coast to the bottom of the hill as they had done during their horsecar days.

By the 1880's, people in major cities began agitating for faster and more efficient transportation. Horsecars were slow, and they left behind quite a large amount of unwanted by-products. The country's first cable car had begun operating in San Francisco in 1873, and other cities were in hot pursuit.

Washington's cable car system cost an astounding $200,000 a mile to build, but it was worth it. Cable cars were fast, averaging between 7.5 miles and 9 miles per hour. The first leg of Washington's cable system followed the old horsecar route, running along Pennsylvania Avenue from Georgetown to Capitol Hill. The next leg completed was the Seventh Street line, which extended from the wharves along Maine Avenue waterfront to the city boundary at Florida Avenue. Washington's cable powerhouse was on the site of today's District Building, The Georgetown cable powered the western section, and the waterfront cable powered the eastern section.

Cable cars were a great improvement over the old horsecars. They were very inexpensive to operate, but they still had drawbacks. The motorman, or "gripman" as he was called, had to stand on an open front platform in all kinds of weather. Occasionally, the grip refused to let go of the cable, which was buried in a slot between the rails. When this occurred, it was not uncommon to see five or six cars hurtling along, bunched up in a row, gongs clanging frantically, while the gripman in the rear car struggled to make the grip let go of the cable. As the cars careened along, the conductors would jump off and race to the nearest "newfangled gadget," a telephone, so he could call the powerhouse and yell, "For God's sake, shut off the cable!"

These buried moving cables gave rise to a variety of youthful sport and mischief-making. One prank enjoyed by "kids" of all ages was to use a hooked wire to engage the cable, and then, holding the other end, swoop down the street on roller skates until some killjoy policeman hove into sight. He put a quick end to these free rides, and often, if the rider couldn't skate faster than the policeman could run, he was hauled off to jail. A favorite variant of this escapade was to tie a piece of clothesline to the end of a wire hooked over the cable and whirl along the street in one's express wagon with a knife at the ready to cut the line and run, should the untoward presence of "John Law" unceremoniously end the enjoyment of the cooling summer winds.

Perhaps the most outrageous misuse of the system, played over and over again, was to take a board with nails in one end and engage the cable by shoving the end with the nails into the cable slot. The board would leap forward and cut a swath down the street like a shark's fin cutting water, scattering pedestrians and causing horses to rear. A favorite variation of this deviltry was to tie a string of tin cans to the board, causing the shark's fin to clatter along loudly as it scared everyone to death. "Foolishness is bound up in the heart of a child. . ."

Washington's cable car days were short-lived, lasting only about five years, when the powerhouse was destroyed by a fire in 1897. Technology had quickly overtaken the cable car, and the city moved on to electric trolleys. Although the age of the electric trolley overlapped the cable car era, it was light years away in many respects.

Frank Sprague, the father of the electric trolley, had built the first electric street railway in Richmond, Virginia, in 1887. His company, Electric Railway and Motor Company, had been founded three years earlier in North Adams, Massachusetts. Electric trolleys were becoming the rage as systems and proposed systems began to pop up all over the country. Even while Washington's cable car system had been under construction, energetic entrepreneurs were busy converting some of Washington's suburban branches from horse to electric power.

Congress, for once far-sighted, saw that the electric trolley was the wave of the future and took immediate steps to prevent the beauty of Washington's wide boulevards from being marred by unsightly overhead trolley wires and poles. It mandated that no overhead trolley wires or poles could be erected in the city. In this way, Washington's underground third rail system came into being. The "plow pits" were at the city limits where the underground power lines ended. The underground contact shoe from the trolley, or "plow," had to be removed, the roof-mounted trolley pole raised, and contact with overhead wires established at these pits.

Motormen finishing their city runs would slowly ease their cars over these pits. Workmen stationed below would deftly remove the "plow" that made contact with the buried power cable in the slot between the rails. Meanwhile, the conductor would jump off the rear of the car, unhook the trolley pole, and raise it so that the groove at the end of the pole fit into the overhead wire. Then, on a signal from the pit crew that the "plow" had been removed, the motorman would begin his suburban or country run. Sometimes, however, he couldn't! The malevolent machinations of marauding miscreants had seen to that. Just after the conductor would climb back aboard and pull the bell rope, signaling that the job was done, pranksters would sneak around behind the car, grab the tether of the trolley pole, and slip the overhead wire out of the groove at the end of the pole. The trolley was powerless, the trolley men were furious. The mischief-makers would run away as delighted with their prank as the trolley men were infuriated.

Problems from juvenile delinquents were minor, however, when compared to the danger from working in the "plow pits." In 1900, the first plow changer had been electrocuted, and later, far more grisly accidents occurred. One obvious and constant danger was that the plow pit crewman would be decapitated by an approaching car. In between cars, these pit men would often come up for air and look to see when the next car was coming. A moment's hesitation could spell disaster.

As the 19th century came to a close, a whole host of electrified lines were in operation in Washington—the Chevy Chase Line, the Georgetown and Tenleytown Railway, the Glen Echo

Line, the Rockville Line, the Brightwood Line, and the Washington and Old Dominion Railway. Battery-powered electric cars were tried on a few other runs but didn't' succeed. One ran to Takoma Park from the end of the 14th Street Car Line at Kennedy Street, a second ran from the end of the Pennsylvania Avenue Bridge across the Anacostia River and up the hills of Randall Highlands to Alabama Avenue. Another unsuccessful experiment was tried with cars running on compressed air. Air tanks with 2,000 pounds of pressure provided energy similar to that of a steam engine, but their range was limited and they were not found practical in Washington.

Dad's first mention of riding the new electric cars came in a diary entry for May 31, 1890. Interestingly, the electrics were his second choice for transportation; he had to use them. His diary read, "Rode out to Catholic University on the Electric Cars. Couldn't ride my wheel—I had a boil." Six month later, he recorded riding out to Tenleytown, ". . . by electric road from Georgetown," to assist in the funerals of two young men from his friend, Mr. Wiseman's church. Mr. Wiseman was pastor of the Church of the Redeemer, a black Lutheran congregation near Howard University.

After first riding the electric trolleys of necessity, Dad soon found himself riding for pleasure. Over the next several years, his diary reveals his increasing ridership. In April 1891, he noted, "Rode out to Tenleytown and to the District Line, where electric cars stop now. . .electric track completed to the toll-gate." He did not say what tollgate or where it was. Other references include: "11/26/91 . . . a progressive trolley ride party." "10/17/92 . . . I went to Mt. Vernon via electric with Uncle Kennedy Butler and other relatives." A week later is the notation, "Mom and Pa and I went out to the end of Chevy Chase Electric road after persimmons but got scarcely any."

By the next year, trolley-building had progressed out beyond northeast Washington, past Hyattsville and College Park. His notations began to take on a matter-of-fact quality, such as, "Went to Cedarcrest on Berwyn Electric Cars for funeral." Shortly after is another entry, "Took Miss Rogers skating at Chevy Chase Lake." The electric trolley had quickly become a way of life.

One very successful method used by the electric car companies was to build amusement parks at the ends of their suburban runs. Chevy Chase Lake was one of these parks, built at the end of the Connecticut Avenue Line. This pattern of promoting patronage from riders on trolley lines was universal in the trolley age. Philadelphia had its Willow Grove. Boston had its Wonderland and Revere Beach. Brooklyn, of course, had Coney Island. All these were run as respectable, middle-class amusement parks. On the Coney Island trains, 75 special policemen were hired each summer to ride the cars as "riffraff bouncers." In New Haven, a ride to Savin Rock on the open trolley cars gave hot city dwellers a refreshing sea breeze before the days of air conditioning.

Washington had several such parks in addition to Chevy Chase Lake. Riders going to Glen Echo Park experienced a wonderfully scenic trip along the banks high up overlooking the Potomac. Luna Park and Arlington Beach were located near the location of the Pentagon today. At the northeast end of Washington was Suburban Gardens, out past Benning Road on the Columbia Line.

In my youth, one of the surest signs of spring was the appearance of open trolley cars replacing the cars Dad called, "Page o' Winter," which were completely closed against winter's cold. In summer, however, the open cars were a wonderful way to cool off, and on many a summer evening, Dad would take Sis and me for a ride on the open cars to escape from Washington's stifling summer heat. Even after our family entered the "aristocracy" of owning a "Tin Lizzie," Dad often took me trolley-riding on the Glen Echo Line. With its picturesque river scenery and unspoiled country, nothing could beat the adventure of riding in an open car. The motorman stood in an open-air cab at the front, clanging his gong; the conductor, agile as a monkey, swung precariously on the running board, seeming always in imminent danger of being swept to his death by overhanging tree boughs. It was amazing to watch him hang on, collect fares, and punch and issue transfers all at the same time.

The open trolleys on the Glen Echo Line had transverse seats with hinged backs that were changed to the opposite side when the car changed direction at the end of the line. The seats ran the entire width of the car with no side restraints or safety devices. Looking down at the ground whizzing past gave you a great feeling of adventure, albeit with some insecurity. Simpler times—fewer lawyers.

Although Washington's third-rail trolley system was quite efficient, there was a price to be paid for the urban beauty. Snow could clog the slots and cause tie-ups. All switches on the system were electromagnetically operated from the car by varying the amount of current. Passing over switches could cause problems for unskilled motormen. If a car's route called for switching to the right at a junction, the motorman had to turn on power while applying a bit of air to the air brakes just before reaching the switch to turn the car.

Trouble often developed if the motorman didn't activate the switch soon enough. When this happened, the front truck under the car would go straight, then the switch would throw and the rear truck would turn to the right. Most of the time the car would become hung with the car heading in two different directions. The motorman then had to go to the rear of the car and gingerly back the car over the switch to get both sets of wheels heading in the same direction. This procedure was always fascinating to watch.

If the car was to go straight, the motorman coasted over the switch so as not to activate the electromagnetic mechanism. If the car did not have enough momentum to clear the switch, the motorman also had a problem, as there was no power at the actual switch juncture. When this happened, the hapless motor-man and his equally unlucky passengers had to wait for the next trolley to come along and push the stalled car until it reached a powered section of the track. In his autobiography, *A Foot in the Door*, Alfred Fuller, the celebrated "Fuller Brush Man," tells how he started his career as a trolley motorman. He was fired from the job when he ran his car over the end of a turntable and ditched it. Fortunately, he was a better brush salesman than motorman.

Another interesting feature of the trolley car was the coast-ing meter or coasting clock. The clock was mounted in a rec-tangular box just behind the motorman, with a tape similar to a cash register. The device measured the distance the motorman traveled without using any power. As a child, I thought that the motorman got a bonus if he saved electricity and ran the car more efficiently. Later, I learned this was, not so! Traction com-panies were not running eleemosynary institutions. The coast-ing clock, the brainchild of the infamous Samuel Insull, was not used to reward efficiency, but to fire any miscreant who used more electricity than deemed necessary. Experienced motormen quickly learned to get their cars up to speed after a station and then coast for the most part to the next stop.

Trolleys, like cable cars, lent themselves to different types of juvenile pranks. One of our milder pranks was to place a .22-caliber blank cartridge on the tracks, which would detonate with a loud but harmless blast when a trolley's wheels hit it. The victimized motorman would stop immediately and get out to see what the problem was. Then there was real mischief—a little grease or oil on the tracks, and the car couldn't get up the hill. Liberal doses of sand were required to fix this situation.

The most fun of all, however, was had with the old single-truck cars. My cousin, Bill Mengert, was a high school cadet cap-tain, and returning from drill competitions, he would muster half his company on one end of the car and half on the other end. On command, each group would alternately jump in unison, causing

THE HISTORIC
Great Falls of the Potomac

Most beautiful place near the National Capital. Park open all the year.   Only remains of the works of George Washington as an engineer: canal, jail, mill and foundry. Restaurant in Park, open year round.   Delightful scenery en route.   40 minutes from Washington.   Double track electric railway.   Trains every few minutes.

Round Trip 50 Cents

TERMINAL: 36th and M Streets, N. W.

"Georgetown" cars make direct connections. For further information apply

36th and M Streets, N. W.   3506 M Street, N. W.

As the use of "modern" transportation became more common, the accepted distance for "local trips" increased.

the car to begin to rock on the single-truck pivot. The more the car rocked, the higher the two groups of cadets would jump until the car rocked right off the tracks! Unfortunately, or perhaps fortunately, by the time I became a cadet captain, all the single-truck cars had been replaced with the modern double-truck cars. Children, then as now, were no angels.

I vividly remember the trolleyman's strike of 1916. The motormen and conductors struck because of starvation wages. With no labor laws to protect the strikers, the trolley companies immediately began to recruit everyone and anyone to replace the striking workers. They hired decrepit old men with canes, dishonest men, men who would not ring up fares, "plug-uglies," and anyone else they could get to break the strike.

This type of strike-breaking was endemic with trolley systems. A decade before in Philadelphia and New York, trolleymen had struck for higher wages and better conditions. Car men in Philadelphia were being paid 20 cents an hour for six-and-a-half days work per week, 10 hours a day. Thus, for a 65-hour work week, their pay was but $12.60. Out of this pittance they had to buy their own uniforms from the company at a cost of $10.00 each. New York's conditions were similar, with the most senior motormen and conductors earning from $13.00 to $14.00 a week.

It is little wonder that men treated in this manner tried to get even any way they could. There were no fare boxes, and experienced conductors learned how to pull the rope attached to the fare meter just hard enough to ring the bell, but not hard enough to advance the meter. Then they pocketed the fare. All too often, working conditions forced honest people to cross an otherwise uncrossable line to survive.

Goethe's immortal words come to mind, "Mankind is always advancing, but mankind remains the same." Horsecars, cable cars, and electric cars were all great advances in transportation. But the human beings, large and small, were still the same mixture of fun and games, good and evil.

CHAPTER FOUR

School Days and More

For me, 1914's most important event was starting school. When Sis had begun school, she went to first grade, as there was no kindergarten in her school. By the time my umbilical cord to the home was severed two years later, the Dent School had acquired a kindergarten. This kindergarten was divided into two sections, high and low, depending I believe, on the age of the children. Regardless of the actual reason, I was proud to be enrolled in the "high" kindergarten.

To walk from our house at 229 Second Street, between B and C Streets, down to Second and F Streets usually took no more than ten minutes if I didn't dawdle. As a teacher, Mother had been a strict disciplinarian. She demanded that her students be on time. Tardiness was anathema. There were no electric clocks in our house, and the clock on our dining room mantelpiece, an old eight-day Ansonia, ran slowly toward the end of the week. Nevertheless, Mom saw to it that I got off to school in plenty of time. When all else failed, there was always the bell at St. Peter's Church, which the sexton rang every hour. On one particular morning that stands out in my memory, I was late despite Mom's best efforts. There were many distractions along the way, and inevitably I found them fascinating.

On the Second Street side of Folger Square at D Street stood one of the many horse troughs located throughout the city. It was a black, oblong cast iron affair shaped like a bathtub. Teams from Zurhorst's Livery Stable on the north side of the square were refreshing themselves with the cooling water that bubbled from the pipe at the end. With childish fascination, I watched as the big horses, Clydesdales and Percherons, slaked their thirst. After they had drunk, the bubbling water looked so inviting that I wanted a drink too. The constantly flowing water was far cooler than the tap water at home, and I knew that horses were clean animals. All I had to do was sweep the scum from the horses' slobber toward the drain pipe at the other end, and the clear, sparkling water was mine. I quickly bent over and lapped up a cooling drink just like the horses.

After my refreshing drink and with the air feeling so balmy, I was in no hurry to get to school—that is, until I heard the bonging of St. Peter's bell for 9 o'clock. Suddenly I realized that I was going to be late for school. I ran down the hill and managed to get into the boy's basement just as the janitor,"Pop" Kerper, was overseeing the boys forming their lines by grades, preparatory to marching upstairs to the strains of a scratchy gramophone. I tried to sneak into line without being seen, but no luck! This was "Pop's" moment of glory.

As janitor, "Pop" had the job of keeping the school clean, firing the soft coal furnaces of the hot-air-system that heated the school, and overseeing the forming of boys' lines in the morning. After he got the heat up and brought order to the chaos in the boys' basement, he would mount his chair on a platform near the furnaces and look out the window at the passing street scene. There was not much else for him to do except to throw an occasional shovel of coal on his fires and to smoke his pipe. His grimy, coal-blackened face made him look much fiercer than he was. Sis had told me how he obligingly sharpened pencils with his pocket knife before the school got a "modern" hand-cranked pencil sharpener.

Pop's kindness, however, did not carry over to his duties in opening the school day. Here he was king. Just as I thought I would make it into line, he grabbed me by the scruff of the neck and hauled me up in front of all the boys in school. "Doctor, lawyer, merchant chief," he bawled at the top of his throaty voice, "and a preacher's son wot can't be on time." Would that I could have sunk through the floor. Before the whole school, before the whole world, he told all that I *was a preacher's son.* I was different from other boys. I was forever marked. Had I known of the doctrine of the celibacy of the clergy, I would have gladly subscribed to it. I was humiliated by "Pop" Kerper, and I would never live it down.

In the past, nice old lady parishioners had patted me on the head and told me, "My, what a fine young little man you are. And I suppose you are going to grow up and become a preacher just like your daddy." I wanted to kick them in the shins and say, "No! I won't!" Instead, I stood by my father's pant leg and didn't say a thing. But this time? This was different. This was school! Then and there, I resolved that if ever there was one thing I would not be, it was a preacher! Here I was, trying to be a real boy among boys, and "Pop" Kerper had made me the laughingstock of the whole school.

When I finally arrived home that evening, my troubles were far from over. Somehow Sis had learned that I had drunk from the horse trough. Naturally, she told Mom, who was flabbergasted that a son of hers could do such a thing. No amount of reasoning could make her see my point of view that horses were clean. She then proceeded with the necessary (in her mind) sanitation procedures—washing my mouth out with strong, yellow Fels Naphtha soap to get rid of any lurking germs.

After I was safely started in school, I was on my own. I didn't mind going to school, but by the end of the first year, I had gradually become aware of my father's vocation and that he was set apart—he was a wearer of the cloth. He was not the same as other boy's fathers.

In the second grade, a new teacher handed us slips of paper on which we were to write various bits of family information for her files. Under "Father's Occupation," I left the space blank. That was a big mistake. She asked me in front of the class what my father did. I hung my head and mumbled something. "Well, does he go to work in the morning," she queried in good schoolteacherly fashion. "No, he doesn't go to work in the morning," I answered truthfully enough. To which she said, "Well if he doesn't go to work every morning, he must be retired." For that year, Dad was retired.

*A*t one point, Lewis Carroll's fantasy, *Alice in Wonderland*, has Alice engaged in conversation with the Mock Turtle and the Gryphon about school and the "extras" they had. The Mock Turtle told Alice: " We had the best of education—in fact, we went to school every day."

Alice replied: "I've been to school every day too."

". . .with extras?" asked the Mock Turtle anxiously."

"Yes," said Alice, "with extras."

As with Alice, "extras" were a most important part of my education. We loved these "extras" because they resulted in having time off from regular classes. Washington, as the capital of the nation, provided many cultural "extras" unavailable anywhere else.

The first "parade extra" I remember was the 50th anniversary of Abraham Lincoln's death, April 15 1915. To my child's mind, 50 years seemed an eternity. In school, when I studied American "Mystery" and learned the facts about the Civil War, it seemed incomprehensible to me that we could be commemorating this event, but the GAR (the Grand Army of the Republic, an association of veterans from the Civil War) was still very much alive.

Then there was Admiral Dewey's funeral in June of 1917. He was the hero of Manila Bay in the Spanish American War, defeating the Spanish fleet and winning the Philippines for America in 1898.

On June 6, 1917, Dad noted in his diary, "The children and I saw the parade of Confederate Veterans in reunion here this week. It was highly interesting." How well I remember that day as the old veterans sprawled on the ground around the rickety red brick buildings at the foot of Capitol Hill in the shadow of that very Capitol they had been bent on destroying. They were lolling around, smoking their pipes and talking with each other. The ever-vigilant fire department was very visible and at the ready in case of fire.

Another reminder of the Civil War was the presence of Dr. Mary Walker. One day in 1918, as Dad and I were driving up Second Street, a group of passengers got off the streetcar at East Capitol Street. Among them was a funny-looking older lady wearing men's pants, a sight I had never seen before. Laughing, I pointed to her in glee and exclaimed, "Dad! Look! Isn't she funny?"

Dad looked in the direction and exclaimed in surprise, "Why that's Dr. Mary Walker, the famed Civil War surgeon." Dad went on to explain that she had served with the Union Army during the war and later had settled in Washington where she had established a private practice. According to legend, she was the only woman authorized by an act of Congress to wear pants.

I was hooked, and this was one "extra" that led to book work. I was so fascinated by this unusual character that I read her biography to help me separate the facts from the fiction. Dr. Walker's medical training, as with many physicians of her day, was sketchy. After two terms in a private school for young ladies near her home in Oswego, New York, she became a teacher. For several years she carefully saved her money and, at the age of 21, gained admission to Syracuse Medical College in 1853. Her course of study consisted of three 13-week terms taught by a faculty of nine practicing physicians. While not the first woman to enroll, she was by far the most outstanding. After finishing her course work, she spent a year as an intern, assisting a licensed physician.

When the Civil War broke out, she volunteered her medical service to the Army, but she was turned down because she was a woman. Undaunted, she promptly enlisted as a nurse. Not until General George H. Thomas, the "Rock of Chikamauga," saw her heroic work in that epic battle above the clouds, near Chattanooga, did she win the right to practice medicine in the Army. General Thomas gave her a battlefield commission on the spot as, "Acting Assistant Surgeon, U.S. Army."

In 1865, President Andrew Johnson awarded her the Congressional Medal of Honor for her service. In 1916, an act of Congress disqualified her, along with 940 others, from having this medal. She refused to give up her medal, however, and wore it every day. I also learned that the legend of the pants and Congress was untrue. Dr. Walker wore pants simply because she was in a hurry, and didn't have time to have her movement restricted by the long skirts that were in fashion. To the end of her days, she eschewed skirts for pants. Dr. Walker was a nonconformist, as well as an early feminist. Once again, an "extra" proved to be of real educational value to me.

During World War I, Dad saw to it that we never missed a parade. The school authorities believed in the educational value of these parades and gave us time off. The thrill of seeing the Marine Band in its scarlet uniforms, 12 trombones abreast across the front rank, marching down the street playing a Sousa march, made my heart pound and my blood tingle. What an "extra" that was. When the Armistice ending the war was signed on the 11th month of the 11th day at the 11th hour, the city went wild. As each division returned home from Europe, there was a parade. Dad recorded on August 12, 1919, "[We saw]. . . a good part of the Marines, Fourth Brigade, which had been in Europe." The following month he wrote, "Took the children to see John J. Pershing, Commander-in-Chief of the American Expeditionary Forces in Europe, who came to the city. We saw him at Union Station Plaza in an automobile with Vice President Marshall, President Wilson being on a speaking tour in the west for the League of Nations."

It seemed that whenever a foreign dignitary came to town, there was also a parade. One event that we school kids found a disappointing "extra" occurred in October 1919, when King Albert of Belgium came to town. Apparently he was not very important, as he only rated our getting a half-day off from school.

The most colorful parades, different from the "government" parades, were the week-long series of parades of the Shriner's Convention of 1923. Dad's diary recalls, "5/31/23 On return from prayer meeting, Helena and I came to the brilliantly lighted 'Avenue' for the Shriner's Convention which begins on Monday." When Monday came, Dad took a total of 24 friends downtown to see the lights and enjoy the fireworks from the steps of the Capitol. The age of electricity had just come into full bloom, and seeing such a maze of light strung along the "Avenue" was indeed an extraordinary spectacle. Compared to the usual gaslights, the brilliant electric display was well worth seeing.

A few days later, Dad wrote, "Margaret and I had seats at the Southern Railway building, from which we had a good view of the parade." Aunt Margaret had obtained the tickets from her brother who lived with her and worked for Southern Railway. Relatives of Washingtonians came from all over the country for this event. The marching bands and glee clubs in their colorful costumes were wonderful to see and hear. Grown men in their white shirts and outlandish yellow vests and green baggy pants, wearing red fezzes with black tassels, tooled around the marching bands and glee clubs in their miniature autos and motor scooters. They were spectacular to watch. Dad, ever the gracious host, ". . . took our guests to the

Washington American League baseball park for the massed bands concert." The week was truly an "extra" to remember.

*L*ike students everywhere, we were not to be constrained by the curriculum laid out by the school board. As children, we found that we had certain educational needs that the regular school curriculum did not include. We considered these extracurricular courses absolutely necessary to properly round out our social, political, and scientific skills. I will refer to the most fascinating and valuable of these unsanctioned extracurricular courses, available only to those of us lucky enough to live on Capitol Hill, simply as "Capitol Exploratory I". This was an elective course open to enterprising youngsters seeking to further their understanding of the federal government. It was somewhat unstructured, taking on the characteristics of an advanced seminar. "Students" pursued their own interests. The course did not deal with the intricacies or inner workings of the legislative or judicial branches. Rather, it explored the basements, hallways, and passages of Capitol Hill.

Those of us who participated in this course did significant, original research into the labyrinthine layout of the Capitol itself, as well as the Library of Congress, the then new, now old (Cannon) House Office Building, and the Senate Office Building. We used the empirical method. We had no drab, dull textbooks or pettifogging pedagogues to spoil it.

The first part of "Capitol Exploratory I" concerned the Capitol Plaza. At the time of the "course," the Capitol Plaza was illuminated not with incandescent light bulbs, but old-fashioned arc lights with carbon filaments. It was the practice of the maintenance men, in replacing the round carbon stick electrodes when they wore down and became too short, to simply throw the old sticks away. We, of course, motivated by our concern to keep the Capitol grounds clean and uncluttered, made sure that these short pieces of carbon did not become eyesores

for sightseers to note. Hence, we followed these careless workmen and picked up all the used carbon pieces they threw away.
The sticks were highly prized for marking all types of sidewalk
games such as hopscotch, paddle ball, tug-of-war, and even
king of the hill. In a word, we were among the earliest fervent
practitioners of recycling.

One rainy day after a long discussion, we reasoned that if
the Capitol workmen were as sloppy in their work inside the
building as they were outside, the inside must be a true treasure
trove. Therefore, we followed them into the Capitol catacombs
for a close look around. There were no Capitol police to bar
our access or egress. Such police, as there were, were quite
indifferent to the comings and goings of innocent-looking
youngsters. The cops were all political appointees. Many were
young men who had come to Washington and obtained these
sinecure politically appointed jobs, while they furthered their
education at night school. They were often studying their texts,
and hence the Capitol was open to all gamin who might wish to
enter.

No one ever conceived of the possibility of bombings or
sabotage in these buildings. True, "Coxey's Army" had *invaded*
the Capitol grounds in 1893, when Jacob Coxey, the mayor of
Massillon, Ohio, had led a band of his unemployed citizens to
Washington to plead for their cause. After camping out on the
Capitol Plaza and finding no redress, the "Army" was finally
disbursed by the Metropolitan Police (the official name of the
local Washington police force). Coxey's unemployed, who
refused to move along were arrested for trespassing on the
grass. From a security point of view, the affair was over.

In all of our tribal wanderings throughout the building, we
never found exactly how many rooms there were in the Capitol,
and we never found all the rooms. Even the Architect of the
Capitol himself didn't know the exact extent of his domain.
One of his reports from the period listed the number of rooms
"at about 526."

In order to support the enormous weight of the Capitol dome, the basement and sub-basement of the Capitol were like gigantic caves hollowed out of solid rock. Massive masonry columns were everywhere, seemingly like the great stalactite and stalagmite limestone pillars in the famous Luray Caverns in Virginia. Tucked away in the innumerable nooks and crannies created by these columns were countless storerooms for supplies and equipment. Workmen seldom bothered to lock the doors to these rooms, as no one would think of entering these forbidden precincts, let alone take any government supplies. We didn't "think" about it. Such thoughts never entered our heads as we played "cops and robbers" or "cowboys and indians" in the U.S. Capitol. What a setting for such a game! Desperadoes hid behind every colonnade and crevice as intrepid lawmen chased their elusive prey. The old light bulbs with their sharp pointed tips, where the glassblowers had finished their job of putting a vacuum inside, were wonderful bombs! They exploded with a *pow* so much more satisfying than the all but silent hiss of our water pistols. A beneficent government could not have created a better playground for its juvenile citizens than that offered by the catacombs under the Capitol.

Perhaps I have done the Capitol police a disservice in alleging they never performed any constabulary duties. "Any" is a very absolute term, and not quite correct. Once, when we were using the well-manicured lawn outside the House Office Building as a football field, a miscue sent our football crashing through a basement window. Almost immediately, the police became the most disagreeable defenders of law and order—running us off and *keeping our football*.

The Capitol grounds, in those early days of the 20th century, were the original grounds as laid out by Frederick Law Olmstead, the noted architect of Central Park in New York city. One of the features of Olmstead's original plan was the "Grotto," described by him as a "... cool retreat during the hot summer." It was halfway down the hill from the Capitol on the west side. It consisted of a hexagonal, arched red brick summer building covered with ivy and wisteria vines and shaded by nearby trees. The "Grotto" gave surcease to the jaded city dweller and weary pedestrian toiling up Capitol Hill. The floor was sunk a few steps below ground, further adding to the cooling effect of the beautiful fountain bubbling in the center. The fountain provided pure spring water, piped from a spring on the grounds of the Soldiers' Home several miles to the north. Here in the middle of a great city, Olmstead had, intentionally or unintentionally, created the perfect spot for summer play. Here was plenty of "ammunition" for our water pistols, cooling water to drink, and shade to rest in. We could play and drench each other to our heart's content. Further, the "Grotto" was far enough away from the Capitol itself so as not to be of much interest to the Capitol police.

One particularly intriguing part of "Capitol Exploratory I" was the electric subway that ran between the Senate Office Building and the Capitol itself. The distance between the Senate Office Building and the Capitol was only about a block, but one must remember that Senators are by definition "old men" and deserve every possible convenience to lessen the strain of their arduous labors. The "subway" from the House Office Building to the Capitol was, by contrast, only an underground walkway. Congressmen, being younger, didn't need to ride! The subway tunnels had been built in 1908, shortly after completion of the House and Senate office buildings.

For us, the House "subway" was not nearly as alluring as the Senate's, which was a mechanical marvel to us. None of us had ever heard of a subway, much less seen one until we examined this one. Here we could actually ride it. The first battery-powered, four-wheeled coaches with solid rubber tires had been delivered by the Studebaker Corporation in 1909. These early cars could carry only eight passengers. By the time we were taking "Capitol Exploratory I," however, a monorail track and a centrally generated electrical system had replaced the primitive

Studebakers. These new subway cars were entirely open with running boards just like the electric street railway open cars. They had four or five transverse wicker bench seats, each of which could hold four or more people.

We were allowed to ride back and forth as much as we wanted and no one objected. This was real fun. There was no fare to pay. At the end of the run, the motorman simply pulled the handles off the controlling apparatus and took them to the other end of the car, which was identical to the first. The backs of the seats were hinged so that they could be flipped over to let passengers always face forward on either run. The close proximity of the subway walls "whizzing past" enhanced the illusion of speed and added to the thrill. Never mind that the ride lasted but a few minutes. It was great fun to board the subway in the Senate office Building and, presto, find yourself in the Capitol.

Perhaps the most exhilarating and enlightening part of "Capitol Exploratory I" came from our trips to the Library of Congress. As one contemplates the hallowed precincts of the Congressional Library, which ranks with the British Museum in London and the Biblioteque Nationale de Paris, it is amazing to think that folk as young as we would be enamored with such facilities for bibliographical research. To many, the Library of Congress was a forbidding place. It certainly seemed so to us as we roller-skated along the walks on the grounds outside. Grouchy old fossils inside often objected to the noise we made, since there was no air-conditioning and windows had to be left open during Washington's hot summers.

In time, the thought came to us: if we could play outside the Library, why not go inside? We entered the hallowed halls by the basement front door on the First Street side of the building. The main entrances, just above the basement door and up an enormous flight of marble stairs, seemed a little too pushy to us. The Capitol policeman on duty just inside the door paid no attention to us as we strolled in, After all, many schoolteachers encouraged their charges to go to the Library to see the Declaration of Independence, then preserved in a tinted glass case on the second floor of the building. The policeman's feet were sprawled on top of his desk, as he read his daily paper. He couldn't be bothered by another half-dozen "quiet" visitors, even if they did seem a bit young to make use of the Library's enormous facilities.

Among our group was my good friend, Skin Dirty, who had been awarded his nickname only after a great deal of provocation. This time, I am sorry to relate, our purpose for visiting the Library was not primarily educational, but to trick Skin Dirty. An earlier reconnaissance mission had convinced us that the Library offered us excellent facilities for getting rid of the livestock in his hair. Skin Dirty, of course, had no inkling of our nefarious plan. He dutifully trooped along with us as we carefully made our way up the inside wide marble stairs to the second floor washroom. It was an immaculate facility with rows of sinks and liquid soap dispensers lining one wall. The attendant, who supervised the lavatory, kept it spotless for his Congressional patrons. He didn't seem to mind our invasion. After all, everyone had to use the washroom sometime.

We then instructed Skin Dirty that the liquid in the dispensers, if applied in sufficient quantity, was the ideal "slickum" for his unruly hair. He was a bit skeptical at first, but we encouraged him—even helped him. Handful after handful was applied to his dark, curly locks before the awful truth began to dawn!

As the soap began to lather, his imprecations and curses filled the air. As only small-fry can, we skedaddled at top speed, leaving Skin Dirty to get the soap out of his hair as best he could. Our visit to the Library of Congress was a big success.

One other area our questioning minds probed, while wandering the Capitol in connection with our course, was the burgeoning field of electricity. The Capitol had its own powerhouse and enjoyed electric lighting, but none of our homes were so fortunate. Though our homes were not wired for electricity, many of them did have telephones. Ergo, we wondered, couldn't we make light bulbs work from telephone wires? We decided to "borrow" a few bulbs from the Capitol storeroom and set up an experiment.

The alleys behind our homes had telephone poles and wires galore. Would it not be possible, we wondered, to put these wires to our use? One of our confederates had a house on First Street, which had a stable facing the alley. Moreover, the stable had a second-floor loft with a front window adjacent to a telephone pole on the side of the alley.

It was a small matter to shinny up the pole, scrape the insulation off two telephone wires, attach two other wires, and bring them into the stable loft. One of our cronies procured an old-fashioned socket with outside terminals. We screwed in our "borrowed" bulb, and we were in business. As the Good Book says, "Let there be light." A dim glow from the low voltage of the telephone wires permeated the dark recesses of the loft. As scientists, we were awed and overwhelmed by the success of our experiment. We sat around in a circle, Indian fashion, amazed at our accomplishment. Undoubtedly, the phone company was nonplused as to why some of its phones didn't work, but that was no concern of ours.

Our scientific appetites whetted, we conducted another electrical project. The large old-fashioned dry cell batteries cost only 10 cents. Hooking four of them together in series to an old Model T spark coil produced wonderful results. Stringing two wires atop the high board fence around the backyard, we silently waited until a wandering feline showed up. Once the cat was ensconced atop the fence, we turned on the juice. The high voltage given off by the coil produced dramatic results. The cat leaped into the air in the general direction of the moon. He never knew what hit him. A confused but wiser cat, he partici-pated in no more nocturnal caterwaulings. Our electric shock therapy worked!

"Capitol Exploratory I" fulfilled the law of unexpected consequences. Not only did we have a whale of a good time, but we learned by doing, antedating John Dewey's famous philosophy of education by many years. These "extracurricular courses" added a great deal to the perfunctory, obligatory work of the classroom.

*R*adio transmission was in its infancy in the early 20th century. Marchese Guglielmo Marconi had invented wireless telegraphy in 1895. He succeeded in sending the first wireless message across the English Channel in 1898. Just after the dawn of the 20th century in 1901, he was able to send a message across the Atlantic. Wireless voice transmissions became possible in 1904 when Sir John Fleming invented the vacuum tube. Two years later in 1906, Lee De Forest invented the audion, or three-element, vacuum tube which amplified radio waves. Then in 1913, Edwin Armstrong invented and patented the regenerative radio receiver that made long-distance radio reception practical. Radio telegraphy grew rapidly; its first practical application was in ship-to-shore transmission.

I saw my first radio antenna on a house on Second Street just below North Carolina Avenue. Strung from a rooftop chimney to a pole in the backyard, it made a real impression on me. Soon, however, wartime security clamped down on civilian radio receivers. During the war, Dad showed me the three 500-foot-tall radio transmission towers just beyond Arlington National Cemetery at Fort Myer, Virginia. The steel skeletons of these towers belonged to the Navy and had the call letters, NAA. At first, my child's mind thought that these towers could somehow literally hurl packets of letters 5,000 miles through the air. Dad quickly disabused me of that idea.

After the war, radio came into its own. Station KDKA in Pittsburgh was the first commercial radio station in the country. It began broadcasting in 1920. My first acquaintance with a radio receiver came through my close friend, Meigs Brearley. Meigs' father was Chief Clerk of the Patent Office. As soon as the war was over, the large bay window in the Brearley's second-floor front room became Mr. Brearley's radio room. Just below the ceiling, he strung four parallel antenna wires spaced about eight inches apart, hooked together at the ends. Porcelain insulators attached the wires to the crossarms. This setup was a marvel to me. How could radio waves travel through brick walls?

A jumble of wires, radio vacuum tubes, multiple plate aluminum condensers, variometers, and earphones were on the tables in front of the windows. Huge storage batteries underneath the table housed in glass jars supplied the power to make the set run. Mr. Brearley's set was a two-stage audio frequency amplifier. The first or detector tube was far more efficient than a galena crystal. A galena crystal was a lead-gray mineral with a metallic luster. The galena crystal detector was the simplest kind of radio set. It consisted of a piece of galena with a fine wire, or "cat's whisker" with which you probed to find the best spot for reception. Mr. Brearley's two-stage audio amplification gave his set range and power that I hadn't dreamed existed. When you put a headphone in an empty, thin glass tumbler, the clear bell-like tones could be heard all over the room. That was the best loudspeaker available then.

With his indoor antenna, Mr. Brearley's set could get not only NAA, but also the Westinghouse station, KDKA in Pittsburgh. At night after KDKA went off the air, other powerful stations could be picked up from all over the country: KFKX in Hastings, Nebraska, and WBZ in Springfield, Massachusetts (now moved to Boston). The wonder of all wonders was that he could often get a station in Port-au-Prince, Haiti. Clear, cool nights with no static electricity from thunderstorms were the best times for long-distance reception. The content and quality of the programs being aired were of little importance to the listener. What mattered was how far away the station was. In those days, announcers gave the station's call letters after each piece of music. In the course of the evening, you could twirl the dial and find stations never heard before.

By the early 1920s, every five-and-ten-cent store carried radio receiver parts. The large tuning condensers were sold by the piece—five cents a plate, and a penny or so for the washers, nuts and bolts to put them together. All the parts, including knobs, spindles, and condenser plates, were in bins so customers could help themselves. Business was so brisk that all a clerk had time to do was ask a customer what he had, total up the amount, and make change if necessary. This, combined with peer pressure led to my mortification. "You can take as many plates as you want," my satanic friends said. "They don't care." Seeing an opportunity for a more powerful radio than my budget allowed, I grabbed a fistful of plates, stuck them in a bag, and presented it to the clerk. Hefting the unusual weight, he sensed that there were more than the usual 45 plates that a good condenser contained and what I had announced. Dumping the bag out on the counter, he began to count. I was a thief! I had far more than I said I had. My friends laughed—I was in tears.

Building my own radio receiver was a big project. I wanted to have a special radio room in the house, but Mom said there was no space. After much thought, I organized "The Lion Tamers' Club," with my dog Shep as the docile lion. Our project was to build a clubhouse or radio shack in the backyard. The shed in the backyard had a lot of wood left behind by the contractor who built the row houses on our block, so supplies would not be a problem. For convenience, we decided to build our clubhouse next to the shed underneath the giant locust tree in the backyard. Dad helped us find materials for the roof and gutter. We even found an unused window in the shed and put it into service. The floor was made of nondescript miscellaneous boards, but so what! It was a real floor and off the dirt. After we finished the clubhouse, Dad helped me onto the house roof through a trapdoor in the bathroom ceiling. He then watched anxiously while I strung a 100-foot, single-strand aerial from the house chimney to the locust tree at the end of the back lot.

Dad gave us his old circular kerosene stove for heat, making our "palace" of a clubhouse complete. It was about ten feet square, plenty big enough for half a dozen boys, a table for the radio set, and our "lion" mascot, Shep. Next, my search for a good piece of galena crystal was on. A good crystal was a "pearl of great price," and I had to choose carefully. Finally, after much looking, I found what I wanted. I made my own variometer by winding wire around a Quaker Oats box. We placed brass paper fasteners along the top of the box to indicate the location needed for the different amounts of coil used for different frequencies. The top of the oatmeal box rotated to make contact with as much coil as wanted. We were in business!

How I hunched over that set, hour after hour, turning the knobs of the condenser and coil to get new stations. Finally, one night we heard an announcer say, "This is station KDKA, Pittsburgh." Our triumph was complete. We had done it. We had built a crystal detector set that brought in KDKA, 250 miles away! Shep sensed our joy, barking at the strange sounds from the earphones. He was a part of all our fun.

"Progress" bit me, and I wanted more. My parents let me use the money I had earned carrying baskets to buy a vacuum tube detector. The detector wasn't too costly, just over $5.00, but it was a lot of money then. Unfortunately, the detector was just the beginning. Radio sets didn't run on house current, though we had gotten that miracle in 1922. Most radio sets were built to use a storage battery. My wonderful Dad went and bought a battery for me at a cost of $15.00, far more than he or I could afford. Now we were really in the radio business.

But the end was elusive. As radio reception improved, I inveigled my folks into putting more and more money into my new toy. Soon it became obvious that the set would have to come into the house, room or no room. There was too much danger of our investment being stolen from our clubhouse. Mother relented and let me put my radio cabinet on the north side of the dining room bay window. It was a sad day when I abandoned the Lion Tamers' clubhouse.

Understanding nature was important to us as well, and we loved the real thing. True, the National Arboretum was located just west of the foot of the Capitol grounds. Its many species of exotic trees and shrubs held little interest for us. Our regular school curriculum didn't pay attention to nature. We made up for this lack by providing our own outdoor study.

The magnificent American chestnut tree is now extinct because of the chestnut blight that came from Asia during the first decade of the 20th century. During my childhood, however, some of these marvelous trees were still struggling to stay alive. My grandmother often took my sister and me to the end of the 14th Street car line at Kennedy Street and Colorado Avenue, N.W., where chestnuts abounded. We loved to throw a stick up into the tree and knock down the brown, spiny burs. The nuts inside were wonderfully sweet. When we had our fill of chestnuts, Grandma would take us to the nearby root beer stand for a cool drink.

When Dad got his first Model T, my nature study greatly expanded. The auto made excursions of a few miles away from the city possible, and we could search for chinquapins, or dwarf chestnuts, as well as real chestnuts. We also made the acquaintance of persimmons, which grew wild. This bounty of nature matured in the fall, and until they had been touched by frost, puckered one's mouth. After the frost, however, they were deliciously sweet.

Another part of my nature study was not under parental supervision. It was carried out close to home. Carrol Street just above our house was lined with ginkgo trees. The ginkgo is a member of the apricot family and prized in Asia for its fruit. The trees were revered in China as sacred. Far more importantly, however, when its yellow, apricot-like fruit gets overripe, it has a most obnoxious odor. Naturally, we named them stinkbombs, and the trees, stinkbomb trees. These stinkbombs made excellent ammunition to hurl at one another in our mock battles or, on occasion, at an innocent passerby.

Another tree high on our list was the catalpa, also a tree of oriental origin. There was a catalpa tree at the northwest corner of Second and Carrol Streets. It was in the front yard of a large yellow house standing well back from the street. In the fall, it produced long, slender, beanlike pods, which we termed "Indian seegars." In our childish fantasy, these long pods, when dried, seemed to be a kind of cigar that Indians would have smoked. Consequently, we had to copy the Indians.

We harvested a good supply of these "seegars" and then repaired to the recesses of our brick garage at the end of the back alley. Dad had built a two-car garage in 1914 at a cost of $600. One side was for our Model T and the other was for rent. The garage was nearly underground at the back end, but the front doors opened at ground level to the alley. It provided an ideal den-like setting for our experiment with "Indian seegars." We sat around in a circle, Indian-style with legs crossed, and lit our "seegars" as we essayed to emulate our imagined role models. We immediately began coughing and hacking. The taste was awful, but who could admit that he wasn't man enough to do what the Indians did?

That, unfortunately, was not the end of our experiment. Every night, while putting Sis and me to bed, Mom came to my bedside to hear me say my prayers and kiss me good night. That night, as I recited my standard, "Now I lay me down to sleep . . . ," followed by the entreaties to God to remember those "dear old folks in the Lutheran Home," aunts, uncles, and so on, I realized that I was supposed to confess my sins of the day. Somehow, in these confessions, I elided some of the events chronicled herein, which a sixth sense told me might not meet with approval. Mother never knew of *all* my daily escapades, but this night she sniffed out my illicit behavior. Mother had a

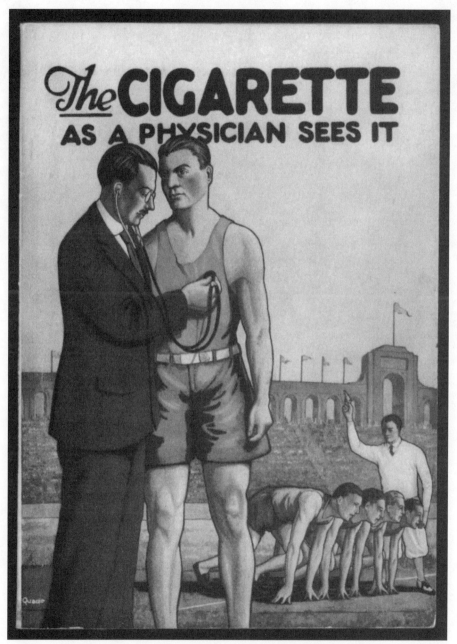

Smoking—anything—was not tolerated in the Butler home.

very keen olfactory organ. As she kissed me good night, she asked sweetly, yet menacingly, "Georgie, were you playing with fire in the backyard today?"

"No," I answered truthfully, "I wasn't playing with fire."

"But your hair smells of smoke," she said. "What did you do?"

Caught with no place to go, I blurted out the truth, "I was smoking 'Indian Seegars.'"

Mother's sorrow was beyond words, that her son could do a thing like that. She quickly left to have a talk with Dad to see what should be done.

Dad was equal to the occasion. For years, he had been an ardent foe of tobacco products. Now his son needed help. Never mind that we hadn't been smoking real tobacco. He bundled me and a half-dozen of my cronies into his car and took us to the YMCA. There we heard Dr. Daniel H. Kress of the Takoma Park Sanitarium give his famous illustrated lecture on "The Cigarette as the Physician Sees It." That was the end of my smoking!

Dad was a pioneering crusader against the evils of tobacco. Numerous diary entries attest to his anti-smoking interests and his attempts to persuade the Superintendent of Schools to put anti-smoking education in the school curriculum. He was in every sense of the word a crusader on the subject. He chaired meetings at Seventh Day Adventist churches, and even carried his crusade to the President of the United States. Smoking, even "Indian Seegars," was not to be tolerated in our home.

CHAPTER FIVE
Tin Lizzie Tales

Dad had his first automobile ride in 1908. By 1911, his brother, my Uncle Will, had a Cadillac, but Dad didn't covet his brother's car; he wasn't made that way. When it became essential for him to give up his bicycle, Dad's purse was small and he thought small.

On May 29, 1914, Dad recorded the momentous event of getting his first automobile in the prosaic way, "After making several pastoral calls in the neighborhood, called at Miller Brothers but car not ready yet." Miller Brothers was a car dealer on Pierce Street off North Capitol Street, and the "machine" he was purchasing was a "rebuilt" 1913 Ford Model T Touring Car, which of course, was an open car. It was black, the only color Henry Ford thought suitable for a car. Secondhand, the car cost $400.

Learning to drive a Model T was something else again, and Dad found it difficult to master. The car had three footpedals. The left pedal was the clutch. With the clutch pushed all the way in, the car was in low gear. When it was all the way out, the car was in high. In between, was neutral. The neutral position was needed when the middle, or reverse, pedal was used. To put the car in reverse, one had to hold the clutch in halfway, while at the same time depressing the middle pedal all the way. The right pedal was the foot-brake.

There was no front door on the driver's side. The body was solid where the driver's door would have been. The emergency brake was just inside this panel and, when set, it automatically put the car in neutral. There was no accelerator pedal. Instead, there was a gas throttle on the right-hand side of the steering column. On the left side of the same column below the steering wheel was the spark lever. Our "flivver" had one other pedal that was dear to my boyish heart, a cutout pedal that disengaged the muffler. Depressing the cutout did away with the back pressure from the exhaust and gave the engine just a touch more power. Without the muffler, the engine made an awful racket and certainly created the illusion of going faster if not actually achieving significant gains. Naturally, I loved the cutout. It called attention to us. But most towns were killjoys, posting signs that said, "Close cutouts." One other essential lever on the Model T was the starting crank, which was located below the radiator in front. Before electric starters, muscle power was used to start cars.

To start the car, Dad had to retard the spark to prevent the engine from backfiring, while leaving enough spark so the gas would ignite in cranking. He learned to set the gas throttle a few notches open, and then pull the dashboard-mounted choke. Since it was inconvenient to race around to the dash if the engine sputtered while cranking, a choke wire was also installed on the bottom side of the radiator. In cranking, this wire often made the difference between "life" or "death" for the engine. When the engine began sputtering into life, Dad ran to open the spark lever to help keep the engine going. When a few straight pulls on the starting crank didn't suffice, Dad would have to spin the engine with the crank, a muscle-building chore that required the complete attention of the "spinner." Tin Lizzies could be ornery.

Learning to drive the car was far more difficult than Dad's diary entry indicated, "Learning to run car. Obtained license to run car, $2." Mother used to brag that Dad's bicycle-riding helped him learn to drive the car. Unfortunately, it didn't help him with the footwork needed. Being cautious by nature, Dad thought it essential to keep his left foot on the clutch for any emergency that might arise. As a result, the high gear bands on the planetary transmission soon began to slip and had to be tightened. Stalling the car was easy too! When slowing, Dad had to keep the clutch depressed halfway. If he didn't, the car would stall below 10 MPH, and Dad had to get out and crank the engine again.

I remember the license plate number of our first car. Licenses then were not yearly but perpetual. The number was 22339, which indicated the total number of registrations since cars had first come to Washington's streets. When Dad began driving, the actual number of cars on the streets of Washington was probably no more than 10,000. Many of the earlier cars, particularly the "one-lungers," cars that had one-cylinder engines, were no longer on the road. Dad never carried car insurance. In the early years, no one needed it. Even in the 1920s and 1930s it never occurred to Dad that he ought to have insurance.

Motoring in those early days was a far cry from the luxury rides of today. In those days, there was no assurance that you would ever reach your destination without some kind of an untoward accident. The day after Dad learned the rudiments of driving, his diary entry reads, "Working in late afternoon preparing for garage." Two days later, he records, "We took [several friends] to ride. Engine stalled in Zoo." This laconic entry brings back to my mind the terror of that occasion. I had just turned five years old, and the car stalled right in front of the lion house. The menacing roar of those great beasts filled the air, and I could see them pacing back and forth behind the bars of their cages just beside the car. How could we escape their jaws? Dad toiled manfully at the crank to no avail. The engine refused to start. Night was falling, and the gatekeepers were locking the gates to the zoo. The importunings of the keepers to Dad to get the car moving were in vain. Stark terror filled my heart. After what seemed like an eternity, Dad's cranking finally prevailed. The zoo-keepers heaved a sigh of relief, and so did I. Somehow, Dad got "Tin Lizzie" to limp to the gate, which the guard unlocked so we could make our escape. Early motoring could be downright scary.

A week after the zoo experience, Dad had his first brush with the law. He, a clergyman, was arrested! His chronicle reads, "Took Mrs. Monroe riding in evening. Got arrested for turning around Thomas Circle the wrong way. Left $2 collateral, which I had to borrow from Mrs. Monroe." Apparently, the strain of ownership was too great for his thin purse. The only way he could escape from being jailed was to borrow the money. His offense was, of course, minor. He had quite logically, to his mind, traveled only a few yards in the wrong direction in order to turn left on Massachusetts Avenue rather than circumnavigate the entire circle. Though he protested dutifully, the policeman was adamant and now Dad had a police record!

Dad's trials and tribulations with his first car were unending. Two months after buying it, Dad recounts, "Had terrific time with sparking of engine. Could only get to the bridge at Langdon." He was referring to the spark coils that were located in a box in the middle of the passenger side of the dash-board, which got wet and shorted out whenever it rained, a common ailment of early Fords. The cure was to install a "master vibrator," or supercoil, alongside the existing coils to boost the spark and make it more reliable. The next month he records, "The car broke down again." This time, he was apparently so disgusted he didn't even bother to say what ailed the beast. He simply left the car where it was and continued on, using shank's mare and streetcar.

Early motorists had to be a hardy breed, and Dad was no exception. Another typical incident was recorded by Dad in his diary entry for October 27, 1914, when he was on his way to the Maryland Synod at Woodstock, Maryland, He wrote, "We left there about 2:30 Tuesday for home. A series of calamities befell us. On Tuesday, the fan got loose (out of plumb), perforating the radiator, which had to be filled every few miles. Plugged it with difficulty with cotton. Could hardly reach Frederick Wednesday. Had a blowout at Walkerville. Got a new sparkplug in Frederick, and a rubber bucket for filling the radiator. At New market, telephoned back to Frederick for new "Vibrator coil," waiting at least one and a half hours, and paying $3.50 for coil, and $2.50 for delivery. We reached 229 [home] about 3:30 A.M. Thursday."

The unexpected could and would happen every time we embarked on even the shortest trip. The only thing to be sure of was that some mishap would certainly occur. Tire trouble was endemic, not to mention engine trouble. Sometimes it was the simple balkiness and cussedness of the car that spoiled the trip. If Dad expected to reach a friend's house by a certain hour, he always added "D.V." to his expected arrival time; "D.V." stood for the Latin, *Deus vult*, or God willing!

Dad was not mechanical by nature, and when winter came, the cold was often too much for our Model T. Two days after Christmas, 1915, Dad noted, "Exceedingly cold, had greatest difficulty in cranking car. Finally had to get Dr. Luce's man Ernest, after working for three quarters of an hour." Ernest's technique for starting the car was common sense and practical. He took a kettle full of hot water and poured it slowly over the manifold. This warmed the carburetor enough to vaporize the gas, and enable the engine to fire and spring to life.

Dr. Luce lived a few doors above us, just north of Carrol Street in a substantial brick house with a curved brownstone lintel over the front door. He was a prosperous physician and owned a magnificent Hudson. His next-door neighbor to the north was Williamson Cook, who owned the ultimate car of that day—a Stanley Steamer. Dad may not have coveted Uncle Will's Cadillac, but the entire neighborhood, my sister and I included, coveted a ride in the steamer. Its power was legendary. It could accelerate going up the steepest hill in Washington. From a standing start at the bottom, it reached a speed of 25 miles per hour at the top. The story widely believed in my circle was that no one had ever dared to let the steamer out to its full speed.

One wintry day, neither hot water, continued cranking, nor my "silent cussin" (that was cussing unbeknown to my father) availed. Nothing would coax "Tin Lizzie" to life. How Dad finally got the car started is not recorded, but the attempts to get it started were enshrined forever in a school essay I wrote at age seven. When asked to write about the most important incident in their lives, seven-year-olds typically have a very limited world view, and I was no exception. My story explained how, "One day, as our flivver wouldn't go, my Father and myself started to push it onto a hill. We had not gone more than a few rods than my first finger got caught in the speedometer cogs. The nail was crushed and the skin badly cut. I could not use it for about a month."

The "extra" of a speedometer on our Ford was hooked up to a large sprocket mounted on the inside of the right front wheel. A cogwheel, which drove the speedometer cable, meshed into the sprocket, thus activating the hand on the speedometer mounted on the dash. As I tried to help push the car down the alley to get to the First Street hill where gravity would take over, my finger got caught between the sprocket and drivewheel. As I had dutifully recorded at the age of seven, it was terribly painful.

The gas tank was under the front seat and held 10 gallons. The car was supposed to get 20 miles to the gallon, but with only a dip stick to measure the amount of gas in the tank, mileage was always approximate.

Yet, with all its primitive shortcomings, the early auto gave city folk, lucky enough to own one, release and surcease from city life. Dad welcomed his auto with all its drawbacks as his great emancipator. It enabled him to get out into the unspoiled country and have the best of both worlds, the excitement of city dwelling and the joys of bucolic bliss. Asking a friend to go riding was to offer a treat indeed. Dad's diary is full of notations, taking this friend and that friend for afternoon or evening rides. He was not only proud of his new car, but generous to a fault.

The Model T was primitive beyond belief. Car heaters were nonexistent. Lap robes helped for the body and legs, but not the face. When we drove in winter, our ears often suffered frostbite. When it rained, we put up the leaky fabric top and put in the side curtains, which had isinglass windows. Rain, however, still got in. There were no windshield wipers on the car. If you drove in a heavy rain or snowstorm, you had to open the windshield in order to see the road.

There was no such thing as a shock absorber, or its proto-type, the Gabriel Snubber, to smooth the ride, and bumps were plentiful. The tires were small, 60-pound high-pressure clincher tires. Changing a tire, a frequent occurrence, meant that you had to jack the wheel up, pry the tire off the rim with a tire iron, try to repair the tube, and get it back inside the casing and back on the rim without pinching the tube and causing another leak. One of Dad's ministerial friends, Dr. James T. Marshall of the Georgetown Presbyterian Church, dubbed Dad's car, "Butler's liver regulator." The lack of shock absorbers and the presence of high-pressure tires not only caused the car to shake the day-lights out of your liver, but also the rest of the anatomy. Even so, we felt that "going for a ride" was worth the discomfort. In 1915, Dad hailed a prodigious feat of travel with amazement— he made the very long trip from Washington to Baltimore and back, over 97 miles, with no blowouts or engine failure. A truly momentous occasion.

Dad's diary entries in July of 1916 were far more common. "Evening, riding with Mrs. Hildebrand, neighbor. Had two blowouts." Two evenings later, he took three loads of people riding, apparently without incident. A few days after that, while driving to Piney Point, Maryland, we had three blowouts. We had no spare tires on wheels, or even demountable rims with tires already inflated. To make matters worse, the early Fords had two sizes of tires, one size for the front wheels and one for the rear. You had to carry two sizes of inner tubes in case a tube couldn't be patched. In addition, you had to have an adequate supply of inner tube patches and boots. Boots were placed inside the outer casing at breaks to reinforce the outer tire. Often, when successive tire failures befell us within the city, Dad would take the injured tire off the wheel, so as not to ruin the tire, and limp home on the wheel rim.

One of the primary reasons for car problems was the condition of the roads, and one of the major contributing factors to Dad's successful round trip to Baltimore was the "modern" Baltimore Pike. The Baltimore Pike was one of the first paved roads in the area. It was a blacktop, or macadamized, road only 16 feet wide, but it was a wonder to me and all my friends.

As late as 1926, Virginia's Valley Pike, running through the Shenandoah Valley from Winchester to Harrisonburg, was the longest stretch of paved road in Virginia. The road was originally called the "Valley Turnpike," and had been incorporated as a toll road in 1836. The word turnpike comes from the middle English and is a reference to the spiked obstructions put across a road in time of war. Tollgates became the commercial counterparts to these obstructions, and hence, turnpikes became roads on which one had to pay a toll. In 1906, the Virginia Legislature authorized the use of convict labor for a road work force, and a small appropriation of $16,000 to be used solely to pay the salaries of the highway commissioner and bridge engineer. In my childhood, whenever we rode through the Virginia countryside, convicts in their striped prison uniforms were a common sight working on the roads under the watchful eye of a guard with his rifle at the ready.

Highways in Virginia and the less populated areas of Maryland were nonexistent. Mostly, the roads were rutted mud, and it is little wonder that the early autos had such a hard time negotiating them. Shortly after Dad's successful Baltimore run, he took a friend to Chesapeake Junction to catch a steam train to Chesapeake Beach. He wrote, "The left front wheel broke down. Lost balls of the bearing and cap. Cost, $1.50." A few days later in July he noted, "All of us motored to Chesapeake Beach. Made 82 miles in all on five gallons of gas. Took about six hours running time. Perhaps half the distance is over very bad roads."

Our "Tin Lizzie" didn't come with headlights or a battery for that matter. A magneto supplied the spark when you turned the crank. The only night time illumination was provided by carriage-type kerosene lamps mounted outside the dashboard. Driving with only that illumination was extremely hazardous. High-priced cars, such as Packards and Pierce Arrows, had acetylene headlamps powered by a carbide generator.

It was on one of our trips to visit Cousin Tom and Cousin Ruby that Dad finally decided to put real headlights on the car. Cousin Tom and Cousin Ruby were not really our cousins, but they were close family friends. They lived in Hampstead, Maryland about 20 miles northwest of Baltimore on Reistertown Road. Cousin Tom told Dad about a garage in town that could install electric headlights that would run off the magneto without need of a battery. Dad decided to try it, and while we visited with our friends, "Tin Lizzie" was fitted out with two new electric "eyes." The new lights were a big success, except that when the car was whizzing along at 12 miles to 15 miles per hour in high gear, the engine was turning over slowly, and the lights weren't very bright. Conversely, when we came to a hill and shifted into low gear, the lights lit up the entire countryside.

On hot summer evenings, one of our favorite cooling-off drives was to cross the Highway Bridge at 14th Street. It was the new cantilever bridge that replaced the old Civil-War-era, Long Bridge across the Potomac. At the Virginia end of the bridge, we turned right onto the Military Road to Arlington. Northern Virginia was open country then. After a few miles going up along the Potomac, we crossed the tracks of the Old Dominion Electric Line that went to Alexandria and passed the Government Experimental Station on our right. We skirted Arlington Cemetery and came to Rosslyn. We then crossed back over the Potomac via Aqueduct Bridge to Georgetown and then home along Pennsylvania Avenue.

Motorists in those days had a camaraderie, a concern for their fellow travelers when a car was disabled. Dad often played the good Samaritan and, on occasion, he got burned. In one week, his trust and generosity were rewarded by losing three inner tubes to dishonest stranded motorists. One torrid week in August, while taking those cooling evening drives, Dad stopped to help several motorists in need. The first man had a blowout and needed an inner tube. Dad promptly lent him one, believing the fellow's stalwart assurances that he would return it. A few days later, the same thing happened. Again Dad lent another tube, which he had just purchased, as a replacement for the previously loaned tube. From bitter experience Dad knew that he always needed a spare. On Friday of the same week, Dad once more obeyed the scriptural injunction, "Cast thy bread upon the waters," when he saw another car stranded with a flat tire, and responded by loaning another tube. Dad was the eternal optimist.

Each of these motorists, however, proved himself to be an ingrate and thief. Each failed to return Dad's tubes or pay for them. In these three instances, it seems that Holy Writ was wrong, at least in the short run. The Good Book says that after many days, the "bread" cast upon the waters will come back to you. It didn't. Dad's largesse, giving away three tubes costing

$1.50 each, put a large hole in his pocketbook. Dad, however, believed all men were as honest as he, and even such outrageous behavior could not shake Dad's ultimate faith in human nature.

With the constant use Dad gave his "rebuilt" 1913 Ford, it was wearing out. Though he had the engine rebuilt, it still ran poorly. Finally Dad saw the obvious and sold it to a more mechanically inclined young man for $100. Dr. Leach, ever the family friend, seeing Dad's predicament, graciously sold him his deluxe Model T with its mechanical starter, oversize tires and all, for $200. What an improvement this new car was. It was light years ahead of our original Tin Lizzie, but it too could be balky, as Dr. Leach well knew. Soon we too found out just how balky it could be. When the engine was warm, the mechanical starter on the dash worked like a charm. When the carburetor became flooded, however, this car could be as difficult as any.

Like all Model T's, when you got out to crank them, there was always the danger of a backfire. One day in 1917, Dad suffered the ultimate calamity borne by many owners—a broken arm from cranking the engine. Dad made the mistake of putting his thumb around the crank as he endeavored to spin the engine. The motor backfired, and before he could disengage his hand, the crank flew around backwards and broke his arm. Dad's diary for the day was illegible, as he wrote it with his left hand, but I remember the incident well. We had stopped at a gas station just east of the Masonic Hall on H Street, east of 13th Street, N.W. The crank on the Ford was permanently attached to the engine. To engage it with the crank shaft, you simply pushed it in and cranked. If the engine backfired, however, before you could let the crank go and disengage it, it would fly backwards. Dad had not retarded the spark enough, and the inevitable happened.

The man at the filling station took us to the hospital where Dad's arm was set. Then, with his right arm in a sling, we began our journey home. I had to work the gas lever under the steering wheel, while Dad steered the car and provided the footwork. While I had steered the car before, this was the first time my automotive skills were essential. I felt ready for anything.

In spite of these vicissitudes, Dad used his car to the full for both business and pleasure. Time and again his diary notes, "With Grandma, all four of us went to Great Falls in the automobile . . . Had a fine time despite some bad roads. Made in all, some 56 miles, returning via Rockville." This entry was particularly ominous for the electric rail lines for it showed that cars could now go as far as the end of the car line and back as a day trip.

As autos became more numerous, there was one more difficulty confronting travel by car. As one wag put it, "Those roads named after that Frenchman, 'DeTour,' are awful." Detours were frequently wretchedly marked and getting lost was common. On one trip to Piney Point, we came upon a road crew putting in a new culvert. There was no sign indicating that the road was closed. We simply came to a big ditch in the middle of a road that we couldn't get past. There was little danger of plowing into the cut because the road was so poor in the first place that Dad was going slowly enough to stop in plenty of time. That day we had to back up and wander all over southern Maryland before we found our destination. Dad likened our wanderings to those of the children of Israel, who wandered 40 years in the wilderness before reaching the promised land. When we finally reached Piney Point, we spent two days at an old Victorian-style hotel where Aunt Margaret and her family were staying. They arrived earlier by river steamer from Washington. Dad's record of our stay reads, "Rate at hotel including meals, $1.50 for Helena and me, each, and half price for the children. Total in all for two days: $9.00." Even with our horrendous detour, we were lucky; on that trip we had no tire trouble.

After Dad's broken arm mended, he continued to use "Tin Lizzie" to the utmost. During the winter of 1918, however, it became more and more difficult for him to cope with the auto's eccentricities. Mechanical progress had overtaken our precious second car in many ways, and the siren song of a car that didn't have to be cranked by hand became more and more alluring. Inflated spare tires, demountable rims, and of course, electric starters were becoming standard. Even so, it was not without some sadness that Dad decided to part with his erstwhile pride and joy to buy a brand new Dodge for $1,001.25. The price included a tankfull of gasoline and the first set of the new annual license plates, which now cost $5.00. Perpetual license plates, which had been a bargain at $3.00, were abolished on January 3, 1918.

The new Dodge was a touring car. It not only had an electric self-starter, big headlights powered by a 12-volt Willard storage battery system, demountable rims, and a spare tire already pumped up, but also a gear shift lever for its three forward and one reverse gears. It, however, did not have a windshield wiper. After several blinding snowstorms, Dad installed a mechanically operated wiper so we could run in bad weather with the windshield closed.

Although the Dodge was a great improvement over the Model T, the original equipment tires were no stronger. Under ideal conditions, they were good for only 3,500 miles and they failed just as often as the Ford's. The demountable rims were, of course, easier to handle than the old clincher tires that had to be pried off the wheels. The new rims had a split in them; a special tool enabled the driver to bend them in and make them smaller, thus making them far easier to remove from the casing. There remained, however, the inevitable patching of the tube, perhaps putting in a boot to shore up a break in the casing, and pumping the tire back up to a full 60 pounds of pressure with a hand pump when you had more than one flat on a trip.

Longer travel was, however, getting better and once in a blue moon, could even be called trouble-free. Dad used the trips to expose us not only to the beauty of nature, but also to our nation's history. Before our trip, Dad had read us a story from

Harper's Round Table entitled, "George Washington: A
Virginia Cavalier", and stories of the Civil War. On the following trips, we were able to see the land Washington had surveyed
for Lord Fairfax as well as the sites of several Civil War battles.
On July 6, 1921, Dad's diary notes, "Trip to Valley of Virginia.
Visited Endless Caverns that evening. Stayed in New Market.
Then 14 miles over Massanutten Mountain to Luray Caverns
next day. Total distance, round trip, 352 miles. Total cost for
us: $23.75." Although the road over Massanutten mountain
was just being built, and hence wretched, we escaped without
tire trouble.

One day, a friend told Dad about Essenkay, a substance
that made tires blowout-proof. Essenkay was a gum rubber
sausage type of filler that could be inserted into the casing in
place of the inner tube. Advertisements pictured a tire with nails
driven into it, covered almost like a porcupine's hide, not going
flat. Six months after buying the Dodge, Dad was ready to try
anything that might do away with tire trouble. He went to
Snyder and McNally, the local Essenkay agents, and had tire
filler put in the rear tires, at the not inconsiderable cost of
$34.75.

Essenkay of course was not a pneumatic tire, and even the
high-pressure tires of the era rode more easily than this quasi-
hard rubber tire. Dad felt that a little harder ride was a small
price to pay for doing away with blowouts, and he became a
satisfied customer. Pretty soon, he put Essenkay in all four tires,
but alas, Essenkay too had its failings. When the tire casing sus-
tained a cut, the break in the tire abraised the sausage-like filler
and caused it to ooze out like sawdust. When that happened, a
flat place developed in the casing, and there was the inevitable
thump-thump-thump, similar to a flat tire. The only remedy
was to stuff rags into the cut to try to prevent more ground-up
Essenkay from escaping. Unfortunately, only the Essenkay shop
had the equipment to take the casing off and repair the damage.
After a few disastrous experiences with this hoped-for panacea,

Dad found it wanting and reluctantly went back to the pneumatic inner tube.

The District of Columbia was well ahead of Virginia in requirements for driver's licenses and license plates. Virginia and the District had reciprocity for automobile licenses, and Virginia did not even require drivers' licenses until 1932. Anyone able to reach the pedals could drive. Dad didn't even have to be with me as he did in the District. Nothing gave me more joy than to be allowed to get behind the wheel of that Dodge all by myself on trips to Virginia.

Speed was becoming an increasing problem as cars proliferated and got bigger and stronger. The speed limit in Washington was 12 miles an hour. Strangely enough, the speed limit was enforced by policemen on bicycles. What a scene it was—a policeman in full uniform bending over the handlebars of his single-speed bike, "scorching," to try and catch a speeder doing 15 miles an hour. When the District raised its speed limit to 18 miles an hour, one of Dad's parishioners expressed his disgust at the city's allowing such an "outrageous" speed.

Maryland, on the other hand, had a far different set of rules, which we learned the hard way. Maryland's highway speed limit was 35 miles an hour, and it was enforced by motorcycle policemen. The laws of Maryland precluded driving in Maryland without Maryland plates. If Dad wanted to visit his brother in Chevy Chase, he had to borrow a set of Maryland tags and put them on the car to escape being arrested. One evening, while out for a leisurely drive, Dad strayed over the Maryland line in Mount Rainier, a small hamlet on the Maryland-D.C. line. Fortunately, children waved frantically at him pointing at the D.C. tags, and he was able to get back to the safety of the District ahead of the waiting Maryland police. Such restrictive licensing requirements did little to endear Maryland to the residents of the District. Maryland license plates cost $.60 per horsepower, an enormous amount. Our luxurious new Dodge had a powerful 24-horsepower engine, and Maryland plates would cost us $14.40!

Maryland's intransigent requirement regarding separate auto registration for non-Marylanders was a thorn in Dad's flesh. It was manifestly unfair to make motorists pay a second registration fee just for crossing the Maryland line. The District did not have the same requirement for Marylanders. It was true, of course, that Maryland led the way in improving its roads for auto travel. Its macadamized roads with cement shoulders were as smooth as asphalt city streets. Because of the quality of its roads, Maryland had the very liberal speed limit of 35 miles an hour in open country. Finally deciding that he had to go to Maryland frequently, Dad succumbed and purchased Maryland plates.

Although Dad was well aware of Maryland's policies on registration, he was not aware of its strictures on my driving. He wrongly assumed that I could drive in the open country in Maryland with him by my side. We quickly learned differently! I was all of 13 years old, and we were on a short vacation to Royal Oak, Maryland, on the Eastern Shore. Dad was letting me drive on a country road where there was little traffic. A motorcycle cop passed us going in the opposite direction, and before we knew it, he turned around and pinched us. We were hauled before a Justice of the Peace and fined $10.00 plus costs for my driving without a license.

The next night, Sunday, our family went to evening church as was our custom. Lo and behold, that same Justice of the Peace was there, big as life, singing in the choir which faced the congregation. Mother glared at him throughout the whole service with her best "schoolteacher's" glare. The man became most uncomfortable and skipped out the back door immediately after the service. Unfortunately, Mother and I were not uplifted by the service. We failed to feel much Christian love for our fellow worshiper. In addition, I was left with a singular distaste for motorcycle cops that has never gone away.

The allure of Virginia, even with its poor roads, was overpowering. In the summer of 1923, on a vacation trip to Page County, Virginia, near Luray, Dad noted, "By reason of heavy rains, bad roads, and engine troubles, we had to stop overnight at Strasburg, Virginia, en route to Luray." This trip, which today is no more than 100 miles and two hours at most, took us two days! While at Luray he recorded, "On the 28th [August, 1923], we drove to Natural Bridge, Virginia, 114 miles each way, the longest single day's run we have ever made. From Staunton to Lexington and beyond, we struck some wretched roads, under construction." Even though we had no flat tires on this outing, when we returned home on September 5, it was another story. Dad stated, "We left the Price's farm at 9:30 A.M. and before reaching Luray [about a mile and a half] had a flat tire. This was the first of seven, which with severe rains, so retarded us, that instead of reaching home at 6 or 7 o'clock on Wednesday evening, we didn't get home until 3 o'clock Thursday morning."

Price's farm was an excellent vacation spot. We could take Shep with us. We could hike up the Blue Ridge Mountains and Massanutten Mountain with the fertile Shenandoah Valley cradled between them. The valley itself was honeycombed with springs and gorgeous limestone caverns that attracted visitors from around the world. Also, since Dad was a preacher and most generous in supplying country pulpits while on his vacation, Mr. Price didn't charge him board.

Price's farmhouse was very modern for the times. With copious amounts of spring water available, hydraulic rams were used all over the valley to pump the water into reservoirs on top of hills near farm houses so that each house had running, potable water. Hydraulic rams were, of course, very wasteful, only pumping a fraction of the water that ran over them. They worked on the principle of having a lot of water run over the ram, forcing it down; the smaller amount of water inside was thus forced uphill. The water was so plentiful that the rams could be used extensively without any cost.

Later, when we read that Virginia was upgrading Lee Highway, Dad decided to give it a try. The route was much shorter than going around through Maryland and West Virginia by way of Harper's Ferry, which was half again longer. Following is the account of our adventure: "We went via Lee Highway over the Blue Ridge Mountains, 117 miles from home to the top of the mountain. The old road was nearly impassable, and the new one was under construction. This road was altogether closed when we returned home, so we came via New Market [over the Massanutten Range] down the Valley Pike. We left it at Stevens City. We had rain all the way, and the roadbed, though graded, was so muddy we had to put on chains. Distance home was 134.7 miles."

In September 1924, when my sister entered Wilson College in Chambersburg, Pennsylvania, Dad noted that the round trip was 226 miles. After this trip he was so tired that he remained in bed most of the next day.

As careful a driver as he was, Dad didn't escape the clutches of the law. In Washington he was arrested for parking beyond the building line at 10th and G Streets on October 1, 1924. He wrote, "I went to a lot of trouble to get excused, but in vain, so at First Precinct, I left $2.00 collateral." Perhaps the reason for his anxiety was that he had had a similar experience a short time before, when he was arrested in front of the Internal Revenue Service office. He had parked there, apparently in the same fashion, while he went inside to pay *eight cents* due on two unused Sunday School excursion tickets. His opinion of the IRS and the traffic police was not very good, possibly similar to mine regarding motorcycle cops.

In December of 1924, winter's chill made travel in an open car so disagreeable that Dad had a winter top put on the car. This was a clumsy contraption that fitted over the body much as campers on today's pickups. It made the car awkward to get into and top heavy, but at least it broke winter's icy blasts.

Though there was still no heater, winter travel was much more comfortable. By 1925, the old 1918 Dodge was on its last legs. The wooden wheels were worn out. The car had 54,000 miles on it, and the lug nuts that fastened the rims to the wheels were just about worn through the wooden felloes. The vacuum tank, which sucked gas into the carburetor in place of a fuel pump, was constantly springing leaks. The pigtail wire in the distributor would give out at the most inopportune times, leaving Dad stranded. With Sis in college 100 miles away, it seemed the time had come to get a new car.

In May of 1925, Dad noted, "Concluded purchase of a new Studebaker Phaeton, paying $1265, reduced from $1,335. Speedometer read 12 miles." What a car it was—a six-cylinder engine that allowed the car to speed to over 50 miles an hour! The car had a hard top with pull curtains like window shades that came down and almost made it a sedan. It had real leather seats, and it smelled really good with its banana oil new-car smell. Day after day, I would go out into the garage and just sit in it for the thrill of being in a new car. I have no idea how Dad financed such an extravagance.

Balloon tires almost doubled the size of the tires to give a far smoother ride. Another innovation was the snubber, forerunner of the shock absorber. The snubber had been invented by an observant, imaginative individual who noted how ship hawsers, wrapped around pilings on a dock, were snubbed to warp a ship to its berth. Using this principle of friction-absorbing energy, Gabriel Snubbers made their appearance in Dad's new Studebaker, controlling the jouncing caused by the leaf springs. They made the ride far better and protected the springs from damage. It had brakes on only the two rear wheels, but the brake drums were so large they stopped the vehicle far more efficiently than those on our previous cars.

The Phaeton body was a mixture of sedan and touring car with a steel-framed roof having a cloth center. The spring-loaded side curtains folded into the top and were ready at a moment's notice to be pulled down and snapped into place. Compared to our Dodge, this was truly a great car.

Perhaps all the improvements on the new car gave Dad undue confidence. The following April he met with disaster. Taking Sis back to college, just beyond Rockville, it began to snow, sleet, and hail. It was one of the worst days of winter. The crowned macadam road became slippery, and before he knew what was happening, the car skidded, hit a telegraph pole, and turned over on its side. The steel-framed roof saved it from turning over completely. The only casualty was Mother's ear, cut by broken glass from the little side window at the rear of the steel-supported top. Dad hailed a passing motorist and went back to Rockville to get a wrecker. Meanwhile, other motorists stopped, and several of them helped flip the car back on its wheels. Its running gear had no significant damage, so I proceeded back to Rockville. On the way I met Dad coming out with the wrecker. He was amazed! Save for a fender and minor body damage, the car was intact. After a careful examination of the car, we continued our trip to Chambersburg, taking Sis back to college. That was a trip we'd never forget.

Although the Studebaker proved its mettle in the accident, the lot of motorists was still not entirely a happy one. Automotive engineering had made quantum leaps since the days of the Model T, but had a long way to go. Tires were still far from good, and tire problems remained endemic. Good roads and highways were still in short supply.

Our Studebaker had one serious design flaw that added significantly to the problems. Its universal joints on the drive shaft were not metal, but rather, three fiber disks held together by half a dozen bolts, three on the engine side and three on the differential end. The play in these disks took up the shocks of the road. Unfortunately, these disks lasted only about 15,000 miles. The constant flexing wore them out, and the drive shaft would then get out of alignment and cause a terrible vibration, making speeds of more than 15 miles an hour impossible. Our

As the popularity of the automobile grew, trips to the surrounding countryside became more common.

universals wore out in Luray. We limped back to Washington at 15 miles an hour, one of the most unforgettable trips in my memory. Added to the worn universals were stripped threads on the rim bolts, flat tires, and heavy rain—a real witches' brew of trouble.

CHAPTER SIX

Growing Up

From the time we brought Shep home, he became a major part of the family. At first, he allayed our sorrow over the loss of Bonnie; later, he became my constant companion. As a pup, Shep's massive paws had presaged the enormous fellow he was to become. As a boy, I reveled in the fact that my dog was the biggest dog I had ever seen. His face was less pointed than Bonnie's, but he had the same tawny coat. He had a little white vest and large limpid brown eyes. They melted our hearts. Wherever we went, Shep went. One day when we were riding in our Model T down Capitol Hill, Shep saw a squirrel. He leaped out of the moving car and hit the ground hard enough to make him roll over and over. Amazingly he was not hurt, but after that, we always took a water pistol in the car. As soon as we saw signs of ungentlemanly behavior, Master Shep was quickly made to think about the consequences with a quick squirt to the face.

Shep was part of the family all through my growing up. Dad's diaries had many entries mentioning Shep, such as, ". . . the children and Shep and I, went beyond Riverdale for arbutus and got a good deal." Or, "George, Shep, and I went after wildflowers."

Shep, of course went on all family outings. When we went to Chesapeake Beach, Shep went. After all, he liked to swim as

much as we did. When we went on blackberry-picking expedi-
tions to southern Maryland, Shep went. He liked blackberries.
Often we would come back with four or five gallons, not count-
ing the ones Shep picked. He had a habit of eating all the ones
he picked! When it came to Shep's birthday, his position in the
family was obvious. Dad noted the following in his diary on
Shep's first birthday, "11/18/19. Today is Shep's first birthday.
We celebrated by making ice cream and having cake . . . both of
which, Shep ate his share." Sis added in her diary, "Grandma
thinks we are crazy."

Cousin Bill Mengert, seeing what Shep meant to me, made
me a pair of shafts and a harness that fit Shep. I could hitch him
up to my express wagon in summer and to my sled in winter.
Shep didn't mind being a young horse and could pull either the
wagon or the sled with ease. Unfortunately, whenever he saw a
cat, he would take off after it, spilling me one way and the
wagon the other. I readily forgave such actions since we were
pals. Often when I felt blue, I would crawl into Shep's box in
the backyard and nestle down with him. He seemed to intuit my
feelings and comforted me with his warm tongue and ever-
wagging tail.

Dad, with his empathy for all creatures, saw to it that
Shep had plenty of opportunity to run and stretch his sturdy
legs, and that included vacations. No kennel for Shep; he
went too. As a young man in college, Dad had clerked in a
highly fashionable Victorian hotel at Rock Enon Springs just
beyond Winchester, Virginia. "Progress" and civilization in
the early 20th century had passed Rock Enon by. In my
youth, it had become an abandoned relic of the glories of a
bygone age. In Rock Enon's decline, Shep was as welcome as
we, and how he loved it.

The old caretaker, a Mr. Lockhart, opened a wing of the
400-room hotel to accommodate a few hardy city folk who
wanted to get away from the mad urban rush and didn't mind
roughing it. Just as Warm Springs, Georgia, had deteriorated

until Franklin D. Roosevelt resurrected it, so had Rock Enon fallen on hard times.

For several summers this was our vacation spot, and Shep and I had the time of our lives at this forgotten ark. The old bandstand was in ruins as was the swimming pool. Though the roof of the bowling alley leaked, and water had ruined one alley, we could still bowl on the other—without charge. The half-dozen springs, after which the place was named, still flowed as wonderfully as they had in the past. There was the "chalybeate," or iron spring; the sulfur spring; another spring that flowed directly from a rock; and ordinary springs with their ornate marble slabs still in place under decaying gazebos, all within a few hundred yards of one another. Shep and I also hiked up the hills to the "Window in the Rock," and even to the top of the Great North Mountain. Rock Enon was a place made for a boy and his dog, and we loved every square foot of it.

At home, Shep developed so much pent-up energy that when we let him out front, he would race up and down the sidewalk like an express train, just for the *joie de vivre*. Once when we let him out, two high school boys were walking along quite oblivious to his presence. He came roaring up behind them at high speed and, for some reason, chose not to go around them, but through them. Books and papers scattered in all directions and the boys spilled onto the sidewalk. They never knew what hit them. As they picked themselves up with surprised looks on their faces, Dad ran over and asked if they were hurt. Fortunately, they were not injured, and when they realized what had happened, the funny side of the episode hit them. They had been run over by a dog!

*W*ashington is not noted for cold winters, but there were some days each winter when we had snow and ice with a vengeance. Once, we were even able to build an igloo in my front yard. Many times, seeking sledding thrills, we went to the

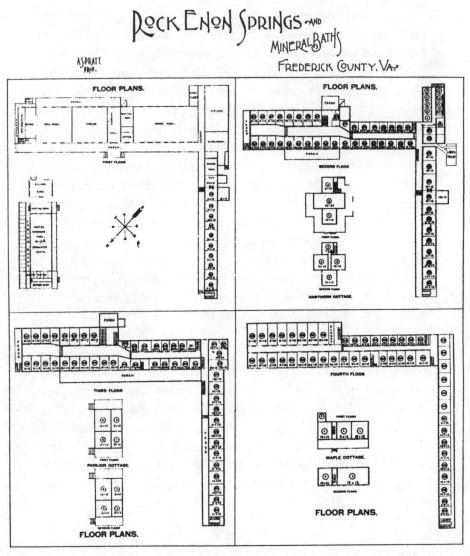

The Rock Enon Springs Hotel had fallen on hard times by my youth, but it was still a favorite spot to visit.

west front of the Capitol to go bellywhopping from the Capitol down the hill to First Street. It was even more fun when Dad had time to tow half a dozen sleds full of kids all around Capitol Hill with his Model T. There were so few cars that it was quite safe and no one was ever upset or complained. On other occasions, Cousin Bill's shafts were attached to my sled, and Shep was pressed into service as a horse for sleigh riding. There were lots of things to do for winter fun. Because Dad had a small church, he often had time to be with me.

One of our favorite father and son sports was ice-skating. Dad was an excellent skater. He could skate backwards as well as forwards, something I couldn't master as a boy. When it was cold enough for ice to form on the Tidal Basin in Potomac Park, the National Park Service would rope off a section that was safe for skating. They would lay planks over the thin ice so that people could get to the safer ice. We were warned not to go out onto the thin ice, something Dad and his brother Will had done many years before when the basin was being built. They both had broken through the ice at the inlet of the basin and had to skate all the way to Georgetown before they could get out of their wet clothes and get warm.

One day, when Dad was too busy to go skating with us, he dropped off several of my cronies and me at the Tidal Basin to skate while he continued uptown to attend to some urgent business. He told us to be ready for him to pick us up at three o'clock, and obediently we got off the ice on time, took off our skates, and waited. Dad was late, and after waiting a short time, we began to look for ways to amuse ourselves. Soon we were climbing all over the statue of John Paul Jones, which was just across the road from where we had been skating. As we frolicked on the monument, we began shouting a popular childhood rhyme at the top of our lungs, "John Paul Jones got a belly full of bones!" This was at the height of the war hysteria that gripped the nation at the beginning of World War I. A policeman came along with a thick gutteral accent, obviously

German, who was determined to show his patriotism. He wasn't about to stand for any young ruffians desecrating the memory of America's first great naval hero. He was about to run us in when Dad showed up. His quick talking convinced the officer that we would be dealt with at home, and we were saved from a ride in the paddy wagon.

After such invigorating exercise, we often spent quiet winter evenings in Dad's study. He would light his round coal oil heater and the Welsbach gas mantle of his desk lamp, while Sis and I snuggled down on the couch and got ready for the day's treat. If we had been good, or passably good, Dad would read to us from *The Youth's Companion*, that magnificent weekly magazine for children that we got all throughout my childhood.

One of the stories that enthralled Sis and me, and yes, Dad too, was "High Times," or "Fried Pies," as we called it. It was our favorite, and we got Dad to read it over and over. The author, C.A. Stephans, wrote of his experiences living with his grandfather, the "Old Squire," in a home on the banks of the Pennesseewassee in Maine after the Civil War. All the "Old Squire's" five sons had been killed in that murderous conflict, and he took over the responsibility of raising his six grandchildren.

The story told of a day when the "Old Squire" and his wife had to be away and left the eldest of the children, Theodora, aged 14, in charge. At lunch, the children loved to play "Fried Pies." To play the game, each person got a pie, one of which was the "Jonah Pie," which looked like all the others, but had a pocket in the pie filled with a heavy dose of a shockingly sour and bitter mixture of wheat bran and cayenne pepper. It was an awful dose, such as no mortal mouth could possibly bear.

This day, just as the youngsters were sitting down to lunch, a stranger arrived and asked to see his friend, the "Old Squire." Theodora apologized, saying the "Old Squire" was away, but invited the stranger to stay for lunch. Theodora explained that they usually played a game with the pies, and it would only take a minute to remove the offending piece and have a regular lunch. "Not at all," replied the stranger, "I want to play your game too."

With some uneasiness, Theodora served the pies, complete with the hidden "Jonah Pie." When each person had a pie on his plate, all took a bite in unison. The Jonah was not in the first bite, so all took a second bite. The stranger got the Jonah! C.A. Stephans tells the rest of the story far better than I.

"Without a word, the bulky stranger sank slowly out of his chair . . . and disappeared under the table.

"For a moment, we all sat scandalized, then shouted in spite of ourselves . . . The table began to oscillate. It rose slowly several inches, then moved off slowly toward the door. Our jolly visitor had it on his back and was crawling ponderously, but carefully . . . on his hands and knees, and the rest of us were getting ourselves and our chairs out of the way . . . The remainder of the luncheon was a perfect gale of laughter."

The stranger told of his boyhood, going to school at Hebron Academy, fishing with the "Old Squire," of the time he broke his arm, and the doctor who set it so unskillfully that it had to be broken and reset again. Finally he told the young people that he had to go, despite their entreaties that he spend the night.

"But Sir," said Theodora, "Grandfather will ask who it was that called?"

"Oh well," said the stranger, "You can describe me to him . . . and if he cannot make me out, you may tell him that he was an old fellow he once knew as Hamlin . . ."

Later, when the children excitedly told their grandparents about the wonderful stranger named Hamlin, the "Old Squire" mused, "Hamlin, Hamlin, what sort of a looking man was he?" The girls described him again, and their grandmother exclaimed, "Why Joseph, it must have been Hannibal!"

"What, not Hannibal Hamlin, who was Vice President of the United States?" shouted Addison, the eldest of the grandsons." Hannibal Hamlin had been Abraham Lincloln's Vice President from 1861 to 1865. What perfect endings such evenings were on cold winter days.

Trains were very much a part of my growing-up. They were the fastest means of transportation available, and like all youngsters, I was fascinated by them. Their mammoth steam engines, belching clouds of steam and smoke, pounding down the rails at better than 60 miles an hour, spelled romance with a capital R. All the railroads coming into the city from the south, that is, the Southern Railroad, the Atlantic Coast Line, and the Seaboard Airline, came into Union Station via a tunnel under First Street alongside the House Office Building. Every night as I lay in bed, I could hear the steam locomotives puffing and panting as they dragged the trains through the tunnel and up the grade of the hill at First Street. Frequently, the staccato exhaust would suddenly escalate into a roar as the drive wheels of the engine slipped on the rails. Then the engineer would have to cut the throttle, put sand on the rails, and hope against hope that he could make it up the hill before he ran out of steam. He could not coal his fire in the tunnel because of a design error that meant there was no escape for the smoke from fresh burning coal.

Whenever Dad had a spare minute, I inveigled him into taking me to watch the trains, and often he would take me to the mouth of the tunnel at New Jersey Avenue and D Streets, S.E. Sitting on the grassy bank at the side of the tunnel, we had a ringside seat as the trains went by. The stones at the top of the tunnel's entrance were begrimed by smoke from the coal-burning engines. It was great fun to watch both the passenger and freight trains come and go. Like any boy, I was fascinated by this panorama.

Also, like any boy, I wanted toy trains with which to play. My cousin, Bill Mengert, ten years older than I, was like a big brother to me. He had a wonderful set of toy trains. His "Ives Miniature Railway Lines" kept the two of us busy for hours.

Day after day I would go over to Bill's house to play trains with him. He had three spring-powered locomotives, replicas of the real life steam engines I loved to watch. The train set consisted of three crossovers, fourteen switches, a signal tower, and "miles" of track. It was a great feat to set up two trains and have them running at the same time without a collision; we had to be quick at manning the switches. One section of Bill's track had a reversing lever between the rails. When it was up, the engine would automatically stop and go backwards. Some of Bill's equipment dated back to the 19th century, hand-me-downs from a friend. The passenger coaches were double-truck but with open vestibules. Passengers were painted in the windows of the cars, apparently enjoying their ride as the train sped along.

When Bill went off to Haverford College in 1917, he gave me all his trains. What ecstasy! Toy trains in my own home. The only trouble was that I couldn't leave them up because we didn't have a spare room. But it was worth the work of assembling the track, complete with the safety plates that prevented the sections from coming apart, to have my own trains. I spent hour after hour playing with my trains. I decided that the most glamorous job in the world was to be a railroad engineer. In my mind's eye, I saw myself looking out the window of the cab, speeding along the track at 60 miles an hour with my hand at the throttle.

My cousin Jack lived in a posh house in the northwest section of Washington. His father was an eye specialist like my Uncle Will, and he could give his boy the latest and best of everything. Jack's home got electric power from the Mt. Pleasant Street Car Line and, as a result, he was able to have an electrically-powered toy train. He had a truly magnificent electric train layout with far larger cars and wider track than my small O-gauge spring-powered outfit. When we went to his house for Thanksgiving or Christmas, playing with his trains was the icing on the cake.

In 1922, when the Potomac Electric Power Company finally ran its lines down Second Street, nothing would satisfy me but having an electric train set like Cousin Jack's. No sooner had the electric service been put into our house at a cost of $25.00 than Dad's diary recounts, "7/25/22. At National Electric Supply Co. Ordered a transformer for George, $7.50." I hang my head in shame—my transformer cost almost a third as much as the electric service to our house! It is especially embarrassing when I note the following, a week later, when Dad took mother shopping, ". . . looking for an electric sweeper vac." Further compounding the guilt, it was over a year later before Dad noted, "The Cataract 1900 Washing Machine came today. Price $155.00 less 10%, through Barber and Ross. It was ordered yesterday, and the demonstrator did a washing, and a big one too." It makes me think that possibly the Biblical proverb should be amended. Instead of only saying, "Foolishness is bound up in the heart of a child," it should also say "Foolishness is bound up in the heart of doting parents."

Little did I realize what sacrifice lay behind the gift of my transformer and Lionel electric train set. Cousin Bill, now studying to be a doctor at Johns Hopkins Medical School in Baltimore, somehow found time to make me two four-foot-long straight-away sections of electrified track out of bar metal. My friend, Albert Jones, who also had an electric train, would come over and race his train against mine. We would set up the two trains in concentric ovals so that his train and mine would run neck and neck until one would derail rounding a curve. Each of us had a rheostat to control our individual speeds. What awful train wrecks we had!

My electric trains couldn't run on my old mechanical train tracks, so Mother, ever the kind and thoughtful person, bundled up all my old set and took it to Friendship House where I know it delighted some youngster's heart as it had mine.

Mother seemed to be constantly cooking special dinners for one occasion or another. Regular family affairs included

Grandma's birthday on New Year's Day, as well as Christmas, Thanksgiving, family birthdays, special holidays such as the Fourth of July, and, of course, the endless entertainment of parishioners and family friends. Dinner guests came from all walks of life and provided limitless knowledge for young, growing minds.

At one dinner party, my folks entertained parishioners, Mr. and Mrs. Cyrus Field Logan. Mr. Logan's father had been associated with Cyrus W. Field of Atlantic cable fame. "Our" Mr. Logan was named after his father's associate. He was a large and imposing man, who wore a patch over one eye. He had lost the sight in his right eye in an explosion in a papermill he was building. Mr. Logan experimented in manufacturing paper from marsh grass, and had invented a machine for "decorticating" it and using the resulting pulp for paper. He formed a company, the Fiber Products Company, which was eventually bought up by the International Harvester Company.

The dinner party with the Logans stands out for another reason. During the meal, we had a small house fire. Mother had an alcohol burner that heated coffee in a percolator on a side table in a recess between the Latrobe stove and a cupbord. Somehow Mother knocked over the burner, saturating the tablecloth underneath it with alcohol, which immediately burst into flame. Mr. Logan leaped up and succeeded in smothering the flames before serious damage occurred, though the tablecloth and table were ruined. For the first time in her life, Mother collected on her fire insurance. As there was no deductible, she received the entire amount of the damage, $25.

Another dinner guest, who stood out stood out from the many others, was retired Brigadier General Anson S. Daggett, U.S.A., a Civil War veteran, who stayed in the Army after the war and completed a long and distinguished military career. General Dagget was a tall, spare man, still ramrod-straight despite his 80 plus years. Immediately after the war, he had been a colonel in command of one of the regiments drawn up at

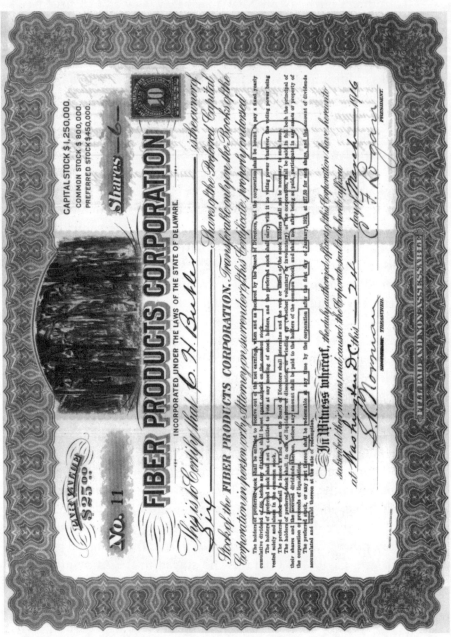

A stock certificate of dubious value in the Fiber Products Company, a firm that planned to make paper out of marsh grass.

the old Arsenal Grounds during the hanging of the Lincoln assassination conspirators. Somehow, time seemed to telescope when General Daggett was around. Dad's father had also been at the hangings of the conspirators. He had been appointed spiritual counselor to John Atzerodt, one of the villains who was hanged. My grandfather walked with him to the gallows. Now, more than half a century later, I was listening firsthand to one of the participants in that historical event.

General Daggett dined with us on several occasions, and his thrilling stories enthralled me. He had joined the Fifth Maine Volunteer Regiment on May 1, 1861, as a second lieutenant. He saw action in practically every major battle of the Civil War, from the First Battle of Bull Run to Antietam, Fredericksburg, Gettysburg, the terrible Wilderness Campaign, Spotsylvania Court House, Petersburg, and many others. After the war, he was sent West to serve in the Indian Wars. He served in the South during reconstruction and also saw service in the Washington and Idaho Territories. He was with Teddy Roosevelt at San Juan Hill in Cuba in 1898, and was sent to China to command the American contingent during the Boxer Rebellion. Although he retired in 1901, he was recalled to active duty in 1904, serving with the Nebraska Militia until 1905.

With magnificent guests such as these as mentors, it is no wonder I loved history as a boy. Yet I remained disappointed that my father was a preacher and I was "just a preacher's kid."

My family's preparations to celebrate the greatest festival of the year, Christmas, were all-engrossing. Entries in Dad's diary for 1915 were typical, "12/11, William Mengert and I went beyond Brandywine after holly . . . 12/20, Afternoon took Miss Beth [my first grade teacher] and Professor Kirby home, with little George. Mr. Kirby gave us Christmas trees, one for Miss Ruth's [his elder daughter] school, one for Miss Beth's, one for ourselves, and two for the chapel." When I look back on it, it seems incredible to picture the way Dad went out in the country after Christmas greens. Time and time again, we went after holly and trees, which grew wild in southern Maryland and northern Virginia. It never occurred to Dad that the worn-out, unfenced, seemingly uninhabited open land, growing scrub pine, might belong to some country person who would resent our cutting trees and holly branches full of bright red berries.

Off we'd go to Occoquan in Virginia or down Walker Road in southern Maryland, past Silver Hill, Redd's Corner, on beyond Surratsville and Clinton to seek our Christmas decorations. Dad, Shep, and I, perhaps a few of my friends, would have a high old time. The fresh country air laden with pine smelled so good. No one ever bothered us and no one seemed to care. Dad said it would be different if southern Maryland had been prime agricultural land, but according to Dad, the soil was poor. It was poor from growing one crop, tobacco, which was extremely hard on the soil. The poverty of the land and its people seemed to breed an attitude of not caring what the occasional auto and its occupants might do.

Occoquan was the place to get rhododendron. Beyond T.B., Maryland (the actual name of the town), was the best place to get really good holly with lots of red berries. The trip home was wonderful. The car was loaded with boughs and trees as well as happy human and canine occupants, all full of anticipation. The great holiday was coming. The decorations were for both church and home. Christmas eve was spent putting this bounty of nature in place for the great day ahead.

For Dad, Christmas Day was a truly religious holiday. A true Christian had to celebrate it as the birthday of our Lord, Jesus Christ. Alas, Sis and I could not get up at the crack of dawn and race downstairs to see what Santa had brought us. Once, I broke the rules and snuck down into the parlor, and was severely castigated for it. It was against our family's code of conduct. In our house, Christmas was not a commercial bonanza. Gifts to the Christ Child came first. Religion took precedence over the longings of a small boy. It was tantalizing to know that the parlor was full of wonderful gifts, and not be able to see them until our religious duties had been performed.

On Christmas morning, we got up early for a seven o'clock church service that took at least an hour. The ride home was another 15 minutes. Then we had our Christmas breakfast with its special goodies—Christmas bread and "kuchen" from Mom's kitchen. After breakfast we had family prayers; they seemed endless. At last, generally around 10 o'clock, the parlor doors were opened, and the whole family entered to see what wonders Santa had brought. Actually, Sis and I didn't call him Santa for very long because we had come to believe that it was "the Christmas Spirit" who brought us our gifts.

Christmas trees in the gaslight era were lighted up, although not nearly as brightly as in the age of electricity. In my childhood, a highlight of the Christmas season was the lighting of our Christmas tree on Christmas Day. We lighted it with open-flame wax candles in candleholders attached to the tree's branches. Our Christmas tree candles were similar in size to birthday cake candles and burned for less than an hour. We had to be very careful to be sure they were put out before they burned into the holders. I don't know how insurance companies stood for such a dangerous practice. Once, Mother's emergency precautions were providential. One of the candleholders loosened and tipped over. In a trice, Mother reached behind the sliding door and grabbed the pail of water she kept at the ready. That plus a wool blanket to smother the flames averted a house fire. Somehow, we escaped disaster!

The torture of expectation was almost always handsomely rewarded. One year in particular, I remember that there, under the Christmas tree, was a brand new Flexible Flyer Junior Racer. It had grooved runners that allowed it to be steered far better than my old Firefly sled. As luck would have it however, there was no snow that Christmas. That didn't stop me from using my new sled, "bellywhopping" on the parlor rug, making believe I was flying down Capitol Hill. In my mind, I steered it around all kinds obstacles on my way to the bottom of the run. Finally, after much waiting, snow did come, and what joy that Flexible Flyer gave me.

Christmas evening was set aside for a family dinner. Mother usually prepared it, except for the infrequent times her sister's two boys were home. When that occurred, we ate at the Mengerts'. When Mother cooked, she slaved away in the kitchen all afternoon. Delicious aromas wafted up the basement stairs, presaging the sumptuous repast awaiting us all. Fixing a turkey was a very arduous task. One year, Dad noted that we went to Newburg in Charles County, Maryland, to get our turkey. He paid $5.20 for the 13.5-pound bird, live. Mr. Turkey then spent the last few days of his life in our old chicken yard. It was quite a chore to eviscerate the bird and then pluck the pin feathers off the carcass. Mother had to use the burner on her old gas stove to singe the roots of the feathers off the skin before she could even begin stuffing the bird.

After the Christmas tree was lit on Christmas Day, it was only relit once or twice throughout the holiday season. Candles were expensive and the danger from fire was too great. One Christmas, a house just a block below us, across from Meig's home, caught fire from its candle-lit tree. The engines from the firehouse next to the Eastern Market came racing. What a sight it was to see those magnificent horses galloping, hoofs and manes flying, a plume of smoke belching from the funnel of the fire engine's steam boiler. As the horses ran at breakneck speed, the wind created a forced draft so that by the time they reached the scene of the fire, steam was already up. The steam boilers were used to power pumps that sprayed water on the fire.

The steam engines themselves were the mechanical marvel of the day. Many feet of small tubing in their boilers enabled the fire in the firebox to convert the water to steam very rapidly. En route to a fire, the fireman on the rear platform had to continually shovel coal into the firebox. During the summer it was easier to get steam up than in the winter when snow and ice on the ground often caused the horses to go slower. Because of the reduced speed, the draft in the chimney was not nearly as good. After their work at the fire was finished and the engines returned to the firehouse, the firemen had to clean the fireboxes of the boilers and lay a new fire to be ready for the next alarm.

As children, we were often reminded of the danger of fire, and at Christmas time, that danger was always in the back of everyone's mind. Dad often told the story of his father's church, Luther Place, burning just after Christmas in 1904. It was a cold wintry day, and the snow-covered streets made it impossible for the horses to make good time as they pulled their wagons through the streets. The combination of slow speed, which reduced the draft on the engine's boiler, and the increased response time allowed the fire to gain too much headway, and despite the best efforts of 12 fire companies, the church was seriously damaged. Interestingly. in 1905, when the church reopened, President Theodore Roosevelt spoke at the rededication of the church. In these simpler times, the president often spoke at various church and civic functions around town.

Many a time, as Dad and I went to the Eastern Market, we would stop at the firehouse and pet those great and gentle creatures. They stood ready in their stalls to spring into the engine's shafts at the sound of the fire gong. A touch of a button by the fireman let the harness fall in place over their backs. With a quick snap of the belly buckles and traces, they were ready to go.

As gasoline engines became more reliable, the fire horses were gradually phased out. The last of these wonderful horses was retired to the lush green pastures at Blue Plains on the banks of the Potomac in 1925. Many years later, when "Old Tom," the last survivor of the Washington fire horses finally breathed his last, Dad was called on to speak as a monument was erected in "Old Tom's" honor. In his eulogy, Dad noted that "Old Tom" was the last of the famous trio of fire horses that included "Gene" and "Barney," who had spent their many years together in service to the community. Firemen who had worked with "Old Tom," along with a group of schoolchildren and members of the animal protection association, joined with Dad in the memorial service. As the monument to "Old Tom" was unveiled, Dad paid tribute to his faithful service, saying, "The memory of his snowy mane and flying hoofs is still fresh in the minds of many. 'Old Tom's' services should teach us to be kind, just and humane to all speechless animals who serve us so faithfully."

Sometimes it was difficult for us to keep in mind that Shep was a dog, even though he seemed human to us. For ten years he was my constant alter ego. What a friend he was. When the time finally came for me to go off to college, I bade him a tearful farewell. He seemed to understand. When I came home at Thanksgiving, the welcome Shep gave me nearly bowled me over. His joy was beyond words. Dad, of course, tried to make up for my absence, but Shep was my boy.

When the dear boy finally passed on to dog heaven, Dad was so moved that he wrote a poem in his memory. It expressed all our feelings toward one who had added so much to our lives. Somehow, Dad's beautiful thoughts assuaged our sorrow.

A TRIBUTE TO
OUR DEAR FRIEND SHEPPIE
(For nearly 13 years, a member of the family)
Dedicated to all lovers of dogs

"Only a dog," said the cynic's hard,
"And he has gone to a dog's reward."
Not so, O friend, for in saner mind,
Your words would have been just and kind.
"Only a dog," you've said, "tis true."
But had you known him as I know,

No words could be found to speak his praise
From very first to his end of days.
Humble and patient, trusting and mild.
More teachable e'en than a little child.
He served with joy his master and lord,
He gave his heart to him he adored.
Is there no place for spirits so rare,
In heaven above, from sin laden air.
Where love ever reigns, untrammeled, free,
To share its joys with you and me?
He's gone, from pain and care he's free!
But did he not suffer as we do?
Did he not feel the weight of the earth's sin?
Pressing without, and perchance within?
Did he not share in creations "groans,"
Had he not oft heard his fellow's moans,
Caused by cruelty, outrage and wrong,
On helpless creatures their whole life long?
Yes, Oh yes. 'tis we know, but too true;
The humble ones suffer as we do:
They share our sorrow, they share our woe,
And ought they not share our joys also?
"Aren't two sparrows for a farthing sold?"
Asked the great Savior in days of old;
"Not alone are they as down they fall."
In mighty power God sustains them all.
"God is love," says the great book of life.
He redeems souls from sorrow and strife:
He cares for his creatures, great and small;
Saves he not such spirits, one and all?
I like to think of this God above,
Who has for his creatures, only love—
Flowers and birds that on earth do dwell—
And must it not be for dogs as well?
How shall we act towards these creatures dear,

Rule them with love, or rule them with fear,
As down life's road together we go,
To give them great joy, or fill them with woe?
Let us remember who made us all;
Who made the great ones, who made the small:
Almighty God, the Father above,
He made us all to dwell in love.
So we trust our friend to God's good grace:
We're sure he's gone to that better place
Which no more knows any pain or care;
Will the Father's love not keep him there?

The Rev. Charles H. Butler.

CHAPTER SEVEN

The Century
Comes of Age

*T*he first inauguration I remember was in 1913 when President Woodrow Wilson assumed office for the first time. Just below the Library of Congress on Second Street, S.E., was a prime marshaling area for the inaugural parade. Regular Army as well as National Guard units came from all over the country. They arrived by train and disembarked from the cars on the tracks lying along the banks of the Anacostia River, just under the Pennsylvania Avenue Bridge. From there, the men marched the mile and a half to Second Street to wait for the parade to begin.

Presidential inaugurations were held on March 4. Unfortunately, the weather was often far more wintry than springlike. Inauguration Day in 1913 was raw and blustery. The troops were cold, clapping their hands and stamping their feet to try to keep warm. Mom, having witnessed many similar parades, knew what to do. She brewed a monster kettle of coffee on the coal stove in our kitchen and had Sis and me take coffee to the waiting troops. They seemed sincerely grateful. Other neighbors followed suit. It was not just compassion; it was the right thing to do. This event was Washington's great day, and we felt this was a fitting way to show our thanks.

The new President was sworn in at 11 A.M. on the east front of the Capitol. After the ceremony, Wilson and his party rode up Pennsylvania Avenue to refresh themselves at a state luncheon. After about an hour and a half, the well-sated and warm President Wilson and his entourage settled down in the reviewing stand and the parade began.

On the command, "Fall in," the troops unstacked their rifles and prepared to move out along the parade route past the Capitol and up Pennsylvania Avenue to be reviewed by their new Commander-in-Chief. After they passed the White House and were out of sight of the reviewing stand, around 17th Street, N.W., the parade ended. When finally told to "Fall out," the troops were on their own. They had had a cold boring day, and their freedom unleashed many pent-up emotions.

The next morning, the paper reported what happened after the parade. In our neighborhood, some soldiers got drunk. They broke into and ransacked Slater's Store, just across the street from the Brent School. Slater's was a favorite rendezvous for neighborhood children, who went there to buy candy. We loved his Tootsie Rolls, gumdrops, and long, black licorice sticks. Mr. Slater was a kindly man, and I was very upset at this vandalism.

Woodrow Wilson's second inauguration in 1917 was memorable for better reasons. Dad, by now the owner of a Ford, had passes to the Ford Motor Company Building at Four and a Half Street and Pennsylvania Avenue, N.W. He had asked the manager for the favor of seeing the parade from the building and received an invitation for six people. Bleacher seats had been installed in the showroom in ascending layers so that everyone in the room had an excellent view of "The Avenue." Dad invited Cousin Tom and Cousin Ruby from Hampstead to join us for the ceremonies.

During the hiatus in the parade, while the Presidential party was having lunch, the parade was stopped. The cavalry troops dismounted, and one trooper, apparently having nothing better to do, stuck his saber into the trolley slot of the streetcar tracks. Boom! A fireball erupted as his saber shorted the third rail. Horses reared! There was great excitement as the marchers scurried to get out of the way. As the fire spread down the slot, fire engines came racing to put out the fire; they couldn't do much until the power was cut off. By the time the excitement was over, it was time for the parade to begin again, although it seemed tame by comparison with the earlier events. I never did find out what happened to the trooper. Hopefully the saber handle saved him from a bad burn. I can't think of anything, however, that could have saved him from the wrath of his superiors.

In my childhood, World War I was an ever-present reality. Despite success in the Spanish American War, America remained essentially isolationist. Before America's entry into the World War, there was a predominant desire for peace. George Washington's dictum, "Beware of entangling alliances," was believed by a large portion of the population. President Wilson mirrored this universal feeling. On October 4, 1914, Dad preached on President Wilson's proclamation, setting aside this day as a day of prayer for peace in Europe. There was little support for America's being drawn into this terrible European conflict.

In spite of these attitudes, war hysteria inevitably crossed the Atlantic and found its way into America's consciousness. My Aunt Grace unwittingly demonstrated just how much the war had permeated everyone's mind by the birthday present she gave me in 1914. The entire country was horrified and upset as well as fascinated by Germany's U-boat warfare, and Aunt Grace gave me a toy submarine. This submarine was one of my most cherished childhood possessions. It was a block of wood, shaped like a submarine, conning tower and all, painted battleship-gray with a torpedo tube in its bow. A lever attached to the conning tower fired the torpedo, consisting of a bullet-shaped, spring-powered wooden projectile. The object of this firepower was a similarly constructed battleship, replete with guns, masts, and cylindrical blocks of wood for funnels. It had a small red button on its side at the waterline. When the toy submarine torpedoed the battleship by hitting the button with its torpedo, a springlike mechanism, akin to a mousetrap, was released, sending the pilothouse, funnels, boats, and guns flying up in the air. It was great fun to fantasize about the real thing with that toy submarine. I was completely oblivious to the terrible reality it simulated.

The atrocities of Germany's submarine warfare were constantly in the press. Public opinion was being influenced daily by the reported actions of the Kaiser and the "unspeakable Hun." The infectious enthusiasm for war steadily mounted, despite the best efforts of those favoring peace. In 1915, Dad attended meetings of the American Women for Strict Neutrality, which called for an embargo on all munitions and arms. A few month's later, as war fever escalated, his diary notes that he attended a great ". . . mass meeting on Militarism and Democracy at Poli's Theatre, arranged by a coalition of a dozen and a half or more peace groups." He continued, "It was a magnificent meeting and completely showed up the groundlessness of the 'preparedness' arguments." Dad clipped newspaper reprints of posters from this meeting, such as, "Don't be scared," and "Do you want to buy a war?"

President Wilson had won reelection with the slogan, "He kept us out of war." Events, however, were quickly pushing America into the conflict. Although President Wilson had coined the slogan, "Too proud to fight," Germany's resumption of unrestricted submarine warfare at the beginning of 1917 pushed America inexorably toward war.

These great and tragic events quickly found their way into the schools. All schoolchildren were given cards on which we were to place "War Savings Stamps." Instead of buying candy, we were encouraged to help the war effort by saving our pennies and buying these stamps. When we amassed $5 worth of stamps on the card, it was redeemed for a War Bond. Dad disapproved of Sis and me for participating in this effort, which he saw as a way of indoctrinating the young into war psychology. My war savings card had a total of 31 cents worth of stamps pasted on it. When Dad voiced his displeasure, my card went into the bureau. Uncle Sam never did have to redeem those 31 cents worth of stamps.

Cousin Bill Mengert, who was older than I, was affected more directly by the war. Haverford College, a Quaker institution, was naturally opposed to the war, but that didn't prevent Bill from working at Hog Island building liberty ships during his summer vacation. The wages Bill received were unbelievably high. He earned $40.00 for a seven-day work week. In the fall of 1917, when Bill was to return to college, he decided to transfer to Princeton, which had an ROTC unit on campus.

The effects of the war were quickly felt in many ways. Two of my cousins, Ulric and Bill Mengert, were now both in the service, Ulric as an artillery officer and Bill in Navy ROTC. At home, the war colored many aspects of daily life. Shortages began to appear in many standard household items. Sugar rose from a nickel a pound to a quarter; regular white granulated sugar all but disappeared from the grocery shelves. "Rainbow sugar" took its place, with crystals all the colors of the rainbow. Kindling wood was scarce and coal was even scarcer. Dad's diary vividly tells the story, "January 25, 1918. Cold, no pastoral work. Spent a good deal of time trying to get coal for ourselves and the church." The next day he wrote, "Several places trying to get coal for ourselves and the church." On the following day he wrote, "Good deal of time trying to get coal but without avail." Dad was not alone. All churches were in the same boat. Three days later he noted, "At Pastor's Federation. Long discussion on churchless Sunday fuel order. Two thirds of the churches were closed by order of the Fuel Administrator. Later the Executive called upon the Acting Fuel Administrator, E.F. Calloway, in a vain attempt to pull strings to obtain needed coal."

As January turned to February, the same futile search continued. Dad's diary for the first of February read, "Cold, but not so severe. In afternoon, shopping with Helena and George. Bought overcoat for him at Lansburgh's for $5.98. Had trying time to get coal. Went to Ferris. He had promised it but finally said he didn't have any. Went to the Fuel Administrator, 13th and F Streets. Closed. Also to D.C. Fuel Administrator, Woodward Building. Then to L.E. White Co., South Capitol and I Streets, where as a favor, secured four bushels at $.40 a bushel. I bought one bushel outside from a colored boy for $.50. This I brought back, George with me, in the automobile." Still again, on February 7, he noted he was once more ". . . with Helena at Ferris' after coal."

Along with coal and sugar, there was a complete shortage of many other foodstuffs. Dad tried to cope with that by going to farms in the surrounding countryside in search of them. In May 1918, Dad wrote, "Took the two children and went to Jefferson, Maryland, beyond Frederick, on the way to Harper's Ferry after eggs and butter. I secured 40 dozen eggs for ourselves, 14.5 pounds of butter. Brought seven or more dozen eggs for Mrs. Smith [a parishioner]. Unfortunately, Helena could not go because of rheumatism from which she suffered severely. For eggs I paid $.30 a dozen for 26 dozen, and $.32 for several dozen, and $.33 for several dozen more. Butter was $.30 a pound." These were real bargain prices! What on earth did Dad do with so much eggs and butter? Some, of course, were shared with the neighbors, who were unable to drive to the surrounding country. Most of the eggs, however, were preserved in water glass, which is sodium silicate dissolved in water to make a syrupy solution. This sealed the pores of the eggshells and allowed us to keep them for long periods of time. We submerged the eggs in this solution in large stone crocks which we kept in the cold storeroom.

Dad records repeated trips into the hinterlands for provisions. Fortunately, though food was sometimes scarce in the city, gasoline shortages did not occur at first because of the relatively few cars on the road. By September 1918, however, "gasolineless Sundays" were decreed. Dad's commitment to God was stronger than to the government and, on the second "gasolineless Sunday," he drove to church. He was not stopped by the police, nor was he molested the following time.

Along with food and fuel scarcities, the war produced animosity toward anything German. When my sister and I were born, our parents had started several savings accounts toward college. Every month, Mom put a dollar into our accounts at the Metropolis Building and Loan Association for each of us and a like amount at the German American Building and Loan Association. War hysteria caused the latter institution to change its name to simply the American Building Association. Another symptom of the times was the elimination of German from the city's high school curriculum.

As the war ground on, and German poison gas attacks intensified, schoolchildren were pressed into service to take a more active part in the war effort. Dad recorded, "Took peach pits to Lansburgh's for Margaret—to be used in making gas masks for the soldiers. There is a competition to see who can collect the largest number." A similar notation the following week records my collection of peach pits. Despite Dad's original opposition to the war, the poison gas attacks apparently changed his attitude. Shortly after the peach pit collections, he wrote, "Went to Union Trust Co., buying a fifty dollar Liberty Loan Bond each for Margaret and George, out of their money and Grandma's."

When World War I broke out, Dad's gardening took on a far more important place in our lives. Practically all foodstuffs became scarce and expensive. Housewives were urged to go to canning classes set up by the Department of Agriculture and learn how to preserve foods. A popular wartime slogan was, "Eat what you can, and what you can't, can." A favorite joke was told about an Englishman who heard this slogan and thought it was very clever. When he went back to England he told everyone, "You know, those Americans have a good slogan, 'Eat what you can, and what you can't, put in tins!' "

Like many other housewives, Mother went to canning classes at a nearby church. In order to have produce to preserve, however, she needed a big garden. To accommodate her, Dad and I became "war gardeners" in addition to tending our backyard garden. We had a big vegetable garden alongside the Anacostia River. This river bottomland, or Anacostia Flats as it was known, owed its existence to work begun by the city as it began celebrating its centennial. Under the aegis of Senator James McMillan, far-reaching plans were developed for the city. The work of dredging the Anacostia was begun in 1903. Great pipes sucked the muck from the river bottom and deposited it behind newly constructed seawalls. The reclaimed river bottomland was to become part of Washington's park system. Our land was on the south bank of the river across from the Washington Navy Yard. The land was ideal for farming. The rich loam was free of rocks and stones, a luxury I did not really appreciate until I was gardening in Vermont at a much later date.

To begin our gardening along the river, Dad went to see a gentleman in Anacostia who was in charge of plowing and assigning garden plots. Dad paid a ridiculously small fee, 50 cents, as I recall, to have the land assigned and plowed. Plots were approximately 50 feet by 100 feet, and we had two of them. One of Dad's diary entries in late March 1917, tells how we gardened. "After attending a funeral, in the afternoon George and I went to the Anacostia flats and began gardening by putting in some peas. Paid 45 cents a quart for Alaska Early." Another entry reads, "Planted 167 cabbage plants. Supposed to be 100 for 50 cents." A week later he wrote, "Bought 50 asparagus plants from Bolgiano's, 65 cents." Three months after planting the peas, he notes, "Got peas for the first time from the garden today."

The devastation of World War I brought on famine in Europe and sharply focused Dad's thoughts on the privilege and value of gardening. Dad was a deeply caring Christian. From his scriptural background, he wrote his parishioners a pastoral letter describing the horrible conditions in Europe. " 'Utter disaster is near,' says Secretary of State Bainbridge Colby in his appeal for relief of European suffering. The expanse of men's minds plowed and harrowed by the horrors of years of war, lies open like a field, ready to be sown with the right kind of seed or with the seeds of poisonous weeds. The world is really at the brink, not of disaster, but total disaster . . . Conditions are too awful to depict, and too horrible to contemplate. For humanity's sake, for our own sake, for Christ and the Church's sake we are asked to help. Sixty percent of the children of Germany know not the taste of milk, and 96 percent [sic] of the babies are born dead. This is not the time for hate . . . Let us give again . . . bread to save the body, and to save Christianity as well, lest in the maelstrom of starvation, iniquity, and despair, all civilization in Europe and America as well be swept away in utter destruction . . ."

With such motivation, Dad gardened away as never before. By midsummer each year, his crops were flourishing. He was raising corn, tomatoes, string beans, cabbage, carrots, cauliflower, and beets. What Mother couldn't can, she gave away. Money saved by gardening went to the relief of war victims. In September, we harvested bushels of white potatoes, and lots of sweet potatoes. Dad truly lived by the proverb—"By the sweat of thy brow shalt thou eat bread."

Underneath Dad's straw farmer's hat, perspiration poured down onto the red bandanna handkerchief around his neck. The midsummer sun made gardening hot work. At the edge of the flats, under a willow tree, within site of the Capitol, was a fine spring. One day, when we came to slake our thirst, we encountered two boys catching frogs from the spring and selling them for their legs. Somehow that cooled our taste for spring water, and instead, when we finished our gardening for the day, we would stop at a nearby store for a soda.

Soda cost a nickel a bottle and was a special treat. We were not allowed to drink Coca-Cola, as Dad believed the legend that in the last decades of the 19th century, it was laced with cocaine. In those days it would have been a perfectly legal way to give the drinker a sense of euphoria and create a craving for more. According to this legend, at the dawn of the 20th century, caffeine was substituted for the narcotic drug. Coca-Cola has always denied the story, but it made no difference to Dad. In those days, we had root beer or sarsaparilla. Pepsi-Cola, first known as Brad's Drink, had been developed in 1898, but we weren't allowed to have that either.

Despite the sweaty, hard work, our garden on the flats was fun, and it contributed mightily to our family's ability to help in war relief. Although our garden was long before the days of Clarence Birdseye and frozen foods, electric refrigerators or freezers, Mother saw to it that nothing went to waste. Despite summer heat, she boiled Mason jars on the coal range in the kitchen, sterilizing them as well as the jar rings. Then she filled them with all the vegetables she could. After the jars cooled, they were placed in the storeroom off the kitchen against the rigors of the winter to come. Thus, our family received year-round nourishment from wholesome vegetables grown in our own gardens.

By the fall of 1918, the Kaiser's armies were in retreat and World War I was winding down. As the world was heaving a collective sigh of relief over the war's ending, another tragedy was waiting to strike mankind everywhere. It was the terrible epidemic or pandemic, misnamed the "Spanish influenza." It was called the "Spanish flu" because it hit Spain with particular virulence, but its ravages decimated populations worldwide. This epidemic rivaled the worst plagues in the history of the world, including the "Black Death" of the Middle Ages and the plagues during Justinian's regime in the Roman world. More than 20 million died from the flu throughout the world. Modern miracle cures, such as sulfa drugs and antibiotics, had not yet been developed.

When the flu epidemic first struck Washington, I was a 9-year old schoolboy. We had no idea of its dangerous consequences. At first, all the flu meant to me, was a long vacation from school; the first way health authorities tried to combat the plague was to close the schools. School closing was but one of several attempts to prevent the contagion from spreading by prohibiting people from congregating in groups.

Churches were ordered closed, a move that brought strong protest from the clergy. Like everyone else, the clergy did not at first comprehend the danger. On October 5, 1918, Dad noted in his diary that the Pastors' Federation of the District of Columbia called a special meeting to protest the closing of the churches by the D.C. commissioners. His diary continues, "The *Star* of last evening said they [the commissioners] 'requested' it. The *Post* of today said they 'ordered' them [the churches] to do so. There was a great deal of indignation among members of the Federation . . . We finally drafted a resolution that we 'cheerfully' accepted the request . . ."

The next day, Sunday, Dad went to his church to post a sign: "Church closed by order of the D.C. commissioners." On his way home his diary notes, ". . . passed the Roman Catholic Church of the Sacred Heart . . . They had an alter on the lawn and were preparing for services there."

A poignant entry the following Sunday brought home the tragedy that the flu was causing, "At one o'clock, at Lanham, Maryland, I baptized three children for Mr. August U.P. Heden. The eldest [living child], Herbert Olaf, was sick in bed, and two other children were also in bed with the Spanish influenza. Two younger children, so far, escaped. The eldest child . . . had died on his 14th birthday, Oct. 9, and after the baptism, I buried him . . ."

After that, the full devastating impact of the flu hit home in earnest. Two days after Dad's trip to Lanham, a neighbor two houses above us died. Our next door neighbors to the south had five people in bed with the flu at the same time—somehow, we escaped.

Despite the terrible toll the disease was taking, the ministers of the city appeared oblivious to the need for the precautions mandated by the city fathers, acting on advice from health professionals. Apparently, the ministers' belief in separation of church and state was stronger than their concern for the health of their people. On October 14, the Pastors' Federation met again, in the face of mounting evidence of the danger, to protest the closing of their churches.

The next day, Dad had to go to the Eastern Market for milk. The Walker Hill Dairy was unable to continue milk delivery to its customers because of the shortage of milk wagon drivers. After completing the errand, his diary notes, "At the Reichards. Mr. Reichard died early this morning. Funeral at Glenwood Cemetery. No interment. Sixty bodies awaiting burial. So many are the deaths, some soldiers are helping to dig the graves there, and I understand at other cemeteries also."

In spite of the danger of catching the disease, Dad continued to make regular calls on the sick. Mother also swung into action, mobilizing the Dent School Mothers' Club to help. The ladies went to to the nearby B. B. French School where they used the home economics facilities to make broth and prepare lunches for the influenza patients and the doctors and nurses who were caring for them. The medical providers were stretched to their breaking point by their efforts to minister to the sick. Dad continued to do his part delivering broth and milk to those stricken all over town.

Ignoring the mounting evidence of the danger of contracting the flu at large gatherings, the Pastors' Federation again met to protest the closing of the churches. Dad wrote, "At Pastors' Federation, we protested the closing of the churches, saying that spiritual forces are stronger than shot and shell. The churches are well ventilated, and the danger from keeping the churches open, if it exists, is infinitesimal in comparison with that which results from keeping the Government Departments open . . . In these times of trial and affliction, it is a serious thing to deprive people of the comfort and consolation they derive from the services of the church."

Dad and the other clergy were actually not oblivious to the danger of the disease. All saw it in their pastoral rounds. They simply felt religious observance was far too important to be canceled in spite of this horrible epidemic. A few days after the pastors' meeting, our next door neighbor died. That afternoon he conducted the funeral of Mr. Reichard's son. On the next day, his diary noted, "Mrs. Brown . . . died about one o'clock today . . . in the evening, did influenza work with Helena."

So the sad saga went. Because Dad had one of the relatively few cars available, he used it to the full during this emergency. On October 31, he wrote in a pastoral letter to his flock, "Verily there is but a step betwixt me and death. How sorrowfully have we been realizing this fact this past month. Many have slept their last earthly sleep; another multitude have been snatched from the jaws of death. But for us, God has mercifully lengthened out the day of probation. How are we going to use it?"

This letter marked the end of the devastation and, by November 11, his diary records far more normal events, "The children had a holiday today on account of the signing of the Armistice. Saw a little of the war fund parade. Evening, downtown twice, to witness and participate in the peace rejoicings. The city went mad."

Thus it was that the plague of war and the plague of flu both ended about the same time. That our family was spared the flu, despite Dad and Mom's repeated exposure to the virus, almost seemed to be an act of divine providence. Dad gave thanks to God for His goodness to us.

The 1920 election was most important. The war in Europe was over, and perhaps more importantly, Woodrow Wilson had stumped the country advocating the United States join the League of Nations. The question was: Would America follow Wilson, who passionately believed in the League, or would it still follow George Washington's advice to beware of entangling European alliances?

Wilson desperately wanted World War I to be the "war to end all wars." To get the nation behind his idea, he had made a whirlwind tour of the country by train, traveling over 8,000 miles, making 37 speeches in 17 states in 22 days. He was not running for a third term, but he was committed heart and soul to his ideal. Unfortunately, the strain was too great for him and he suffered a stroke. His illness doomed whatever chance the treaty had, and next year's Democratic standard bearer, James M. Cox, never made the same commitment.

On November 2, 1920, Dad wrote in his diary, "Evening, all four of us went down town to hear election results." They were flashed on a screen on the front of the *Post* building and broadcast over a loudspeaker for all to hear. Dad noted, "It was all one way, save for the solid south." Warren G. Harding won by a landslide, and his comment sounded the League's demise, "The league is now a closed incident." His inauguration the following year was marked by two breaks with tradition. His speech was the first inaugural address amplified by loudspeaker so everyone in the vast throng could hear him. Interestingly, too, Harding decreed that the usual military parade accompanying the inaugural would be omitted. The nation had had enough of war.

*D*ad had been a supporter of women's rights since 1891 when he attended the "First Triennial Meeting of the Women's National Council." Over the course of time, the movement had gone through rollercoaster rides of successes and failures. Women's rights, however would not stay dead. In my early childhood I remember the Woman's Suffrage

Headquarters on First Street, N.E., opposite the Capitol grounds. By 1915, at the opening of Congress, Dad reported, "There was a march of woman suffragists to the Capitol where they presented to Senator George Sutherland of Utah and Representative Mondell of Wyoming a monster petition of 400,000 or more names for woman's suffrage."

In 1917, women had still been denied the right to vote, and many ". . . ladies of wealth and distinction," as the *Washington Post* put it, had been imprisoned in the workhouse at Occaquan, Virginia, for daring to demand their right to vote. The irony of America fighting a war to ". . . make the world safe for democracy," had not been lost on them or on my father.

In 1920, the agitation of the suffragists and their supporters finally bore fruit with the ratification of the 19th, or Women's Suffrage Amendment to the Constitution. Women now had the right to vote. Times were indeed changing.

As times changed, the types of people visiting the nation's capital changed with them. One of my most unforgettable experiences was hearing and seeing Billy Sunday preach. Sunday was the famed Chicago White Sox baseball player turned evangelist. Dad had been among a group of 79 Washington clergymen who traveled to Philadelphia to importune Sunday to come to Washington and conduct an evangelistic campaign. Sunday equivocated. He would only come, if at all, when Congress was in session. Finally, in January 1918, he came. Before opening his crusade, he met with the local clergy at the First Congregational Church and asked for money. Dad subscribed $5, which he really could ill afford.

A great wooden Liberty Hut had been built on Union Plaza during the war. It was shaped as a large amphitheater with bleacher seats rising on all sides. The podium was at ground level in the middle. This was to become Sunday's tabernacle.

Sunday put on a spellbinding performance. He took off his coat and tie right in front of the assembled worshipers, and literally wrestled with the devil. He shouted, "I hate sin! I'll fight sin until hell freezes over, and then I'll go after it on ice skates!" Under the spell of such colorful antics and oratory, many listeners were converted. After a year of this, however, Dad, as well as many others, became thoroughly disillusioned with Sunday's outrageous antics and blasphemous prayers. Very few of the local clergy were sad to see him finally leave.

A host of other celebrities toured American cities in those days, and Washington was a stop for almost all of them. Some of the more memorable we saw included Howard Thurston, the great magician; Helen Keller, the famous blind and deaf leader who spoke in the Washington Auditorium; Harry Houdini, the king of all magicians who presented his famous expose of spiritualism; and Bertrand Russell, the future Nobel Prize winner, English philosopher, mathematician, author, and pacifist, who spoke at the City Club under the auspices of the League for Social Democracy. I also will never forget Commander Richard Evelyn Byrd's reception after his historic flight over the North Pole. As a child, I couldn't understand why such a heroic figure had a "girl's" name, until Dad explained that Evelyn was a family name.

One of the biggest days of my youth was the day Charles A. Lindbergh was welcomed home after his daring and magnificent solo flight across the Atlantic. Dad's diary entry describes it well, "The day was cloudy but warm. This was a day of great excitement because President Coolidge was to honor Colonel Lindbergh for his wonderful transatlantic flight. The city was thronged with people and automobiles. All of us saw the U.S.S. *Memphis* come up to the Navy Yard. We were at the pier of the garbage disposal plant at the foot of Second Street." Dad, who knew the city well, thought this pier would afford a good vantage point, not nearly so crowded as the Navy Yard. He was right. We saw Lindbergh, bare-headed, standing on the foredeck of the *Memphis*, waving to the cheering throngs and the tumultuous welcome that greeted him. All in all, Washington's social and cultural life was outstanding; Washingtonians had the opportunity to participate in history in the making.

Bands always held a fascination for me. It never ceased to be a thrill for me to see the U.S. Marine Band marching down the street in Washington's many parades. They marched in perfect time and formation to many of the most glorious of Sousa's marches—*Semper Fidelis*, *The Washington Post*, or *The Stars and Stripes Forever*, to name but a few. The stirring music never failed to send chills up and down my spine.

To be able to play in a band was one of my fondest dreams. When I entered Eastern High School in 1923, there was no band. The school had an orchestra, but bands were not part of the school's curriculum. I played the violin, but desperately wanted to play a band instrument. Determinedly, I canvassed the wind section of the school orchestra. There were a couple of cornets, a clarinet, and even a French horn player interested, but not quite enough for a real band. In desperation, I got out Dad's old "sawed-off" Disston cornet and tried to blow it. I coaxed out a few notes but it just wouldn't work. It was the worst horn I have ever tried to play. My ever-indulgent parents, sensing my determination, let me trade that old cornet for a used trumpet at Droops' Music Store. This old, silvered trumpet had half the silver plate worn off, but it was far easier to blow. I had to learn to read cornet music on my own, which was a note different from violin scores, but that was easy.

Unfortunately, adding another cornet didn't help much as far as the band was concerned. What we needed was some lower brass. Luckily, my best friend in high school, Conrad "Bud" Grohs, played the trombone and found a way to help. His father was a fine B-flat bass player. He was also instrument custodian for the Almas Temple Shrine Band. When Bud told him of our dilemma, he agreed to help. He had an old baritone horn in good condition with a fine tone, dating from the 19th century. It was not being used, so he traded it to me for my trumpet. It was a Frank Holton baritone, one of the best of its day. The horn was an old high-pitch instrument, but it had a low-pitch shank, and by pulling the slides of the first and third valves out a little way, it came into perfect tune with standard concert-pitch instruments.

The first night Bud brought that baritone over to our house, Mother was upstairs with one of her splitting migraine headaches. Bud and I were playing in the second-floor parlor, and when the sound of that beautifully toned, mellow baritone reached Mom, she said it actually soothed her headache. I fell in love with it immediately and quickly mastered the bass clef. I also had to develop the embouchure needed for the lower octave of the baritone.

The baritone's sound was pure honey, and best of all, I got to play the countermelody that stood out. With Bud's trombone and my baritone, our young band began to get some body. We had Ronald Brown's clarinet leading the woodwinds; Herbert Cooper's fine cornet work gave us a good soprano lead. "Frenchie" Duvall's French Horn, a sax or two, and of course, percussion gave us the start of a very decent band.

The school authorities, seeing how earnest we were, decided to give us professional help. Once a week, Mr. Ludwig Manoly came to coach our new band. On those occasions, we played in the school auditorium during lunch hour to entertain students after they finished lunch. We were doing pretty well, but still needed a bass player. When one of the Bush boys came back to school after a short stint with the Marine Band, we had our bass player. Then we sounded like a real band.

There was, however, more to life than music. In 1924, the Washington Nationals, Clark Griffith's American League baseball team, won the league championship for the first time in the team's history. The town went wild. Walter Johnson, the famed "Big Train" fastball pitcher of the "Nats," was the hero of every boy in town. He and Herold "Muddy" Ruel, a lawyer in the off-season (the papers always referred to him as Walter's "barrister catcher"}, were the finest battery in baseball. Muddy was a .300 hitter. Johnson's tragedy was that, throughout his long years with the "Nats," he had always had a second-rate team behind him and had never been able to get to the World Series. Now, near the twilight of his career, he finally had made it. He was the strikeout king of baseball. Earlier in his career, he had hurled three consecutive shutout games against the New York Highlanders, the precursor team before the Yankees.

Dad, like all preachers then, received a pass to all regular-season American League games in Washington from Mr. Griffith. The best part of the pass was that Dad could take along with him as many small-fry as he wished. In this, Dad was a real hero to us—that is, Meigs, "Bones," "Skin Dirty" and all the rest. It also made us real fans of the game. How Dad found time to take us to ball games, pastor a growing congregation, teach on the faculty of Howard University Divinity School, and take on his gardening and regular chores, I've never understood. But he did, and "Skin Dirty," unable to believe that fathers spent time with their families, actually believed that he was my elder brother.

Before the days of radio, I, together with many other urchins, large and small, had gone to "The Avenue" at 4th Street and watched as the scores were posted inning by inning on a scoreboard over a one-floor storefront. Now for the 1924 World Series, I could listen on my own radio in rapt attention, albeit agonizingly, to the game, pitch by pitch, out by out. What torture! In the first game, John McGraw's Giants beat Walter Johnson and the "Nats." A couple of days later, the same horrendous thing happened. Everyone wondered, "Was the 'Big Train' too old? Had his chance at the World Series come too late?"

Somehow, my beloved Nationals struggled back and tied the series at three games apiece. The final and deciding game was to be in Washington. There were no free tickets here; I sat transfixed at my radio. With the score tied in the ninth inning, the ultimate occurred—Walter Johnson was called in to pitch!

Commentators and announcers alike asked, "Could he do it? Could he win the game? Is the grand old man of baseball 'over the hill'?" The wisemen of radio advised it was murder to put him in again. After all, he had been beaten in his first two starts.

The headphones of my radio were glued to my ears. After what seemed like an eternity, Johnson got the Giants out in the 10th, and then again in the 11th. But the "Nats" were equally impotent. They couldn't do a thing with McGraw's minions. Then finally came the 12th. I prayed, "Lord, give Walter strength to win." Once more he got through the inning; the terrible Giants were unable to score. Then, the miracle happened. Washington scored in the bottom of the 12th, *Washington had won its first World Series championship.*

Back in high school, I had been steadily rising through the ranks of the High School Cadet Corps. The corps was a highly prestigious organization, and becoming a Cadet Captain in your senior year was one of the highest honors the school could bestow upon you. Ten years before my time, my Cousin Bill became a Cadet Captain, and nothing less would do for me. Each year as I rose through the ranks, I had that one goal in mind. Cadet officers were chosen both on academic achievement and proficiency in drill. By the time my senior year came around, Eastern's six companies in two battalions had shrunk to one battalion and four companies. I anguished. Would I be selected as one of the four captains? I went to the Government Printing Office and got all the pamphlets I could find on close order drill and studied them diligently in preparation for the exam.

When school started in the fall of 1926, all prospective officers sat down and took the test. Then there was a week of nightmarish waiting. Finally, all the candidates were assembled in the drill room and the results were announced. I had made it! I rushed to the school pay phone and called Mom. "This is Captain Butler speaking," I fairly shouted into the mouthpiece; I was so happy. I was no longer just "the preacher's kid." I had status. I felt it was the greatest thing that had ever happened to me.

I quickly learned the name of every boy in my company. Every time I saw one, I greeted him by name. Such attention paid off, and by late fall, my company, Company "C," was the best company at Eastern High. The high point of the year for the corps was the annual city-wide competitive drill held in Griffith Stadium. Winning that drill entitled members of the winning company to wear a red diamond on the left sleeve of their uniforms, denoting their excellence. Cousin Bill's company had won the competition the year before he was a Cadet Captain; now it was my turn.

I continued to work toward that ultimate goal. We drilled and drilled. On February 7, Dad noted in his diary, "In afternoon, Helena and I saw High School Cadets drill a little. (An inspection which George's Company C won.)" A few days later, Dad wrote, "2/18, great preparation party in High School Armory for George's Cadet Company. Went to Holzbeierlein's Bakery for four loaves of Pullman bread for tonight. Picked up cakes from several mothers. Borrowed game books from Miss Stockett [a teacher mother knew from her teaching days]. I counted 43 boys, and in addition eight or ten grownups."

In April, I had 11 of my cadet officers and NCOs over for an evening of fun. We were working hard, and I wanted to spare no effort to instill that extra bit of *esprit de corps*. The competition was in May, and time was running out. Just before the competition, my Cousin Bill came over from Johns Hopkins in Baltimore, where he was studying medicine, especially to see my company drill. Dad even brought a family friend and military authority, General Anson S. Daggett of Civil War fame, to see my company as well as the others perform.

To further promote company spirit, I got armbands with a big "C" on them for girls to wear and become company boosters. Company C was riding high. As the competition approached, company morale soared and we had great hopes of winning the coveted trophy for the school.

On the afternoon of the last day, Company C was chosen to be an exhibition company, one of the five to compete, before the brigade marched in to learn who had won. As the Cadet Band from Central High played *The Washington Post March*, we marched onto the field in perfect formation, wheeled into line before the judges in excellent dress, and reported. Then, disaster struck! It was raining and the rifles were slippery. Two members of my company dropped their rifles. It was over, we had lost. The victory supper planned at Eastern was canceled. The 60 chairs on the stage remained empty.

Although my company did not win the coveted honor of being the best in the city, being a Captain was the most important thing that happened to me in high school. I was respected by my peers, and in my mind, I was no longer "just a preacher's kid." At graduation a few weeks later, the school bestowed its gold alumni medal on me as *Primus Schola Orientalis* or First Scholar of Eastern. My childhood day's, growing up in the city, were over.

Ashamed of
My Best

No son could ever have had a father more kind, consid-
erate, and loving than I. He was my constant
companion and helper as I grew up. Yet, as I began to go to
school, I became aware that my father was different from
other boys' fathers—he was a minister. He didn't wear
"preacher clothes," such as clerical collars or vestments, but
he was different from my friends' fathers. I got it into my head
that being a preacher's son made me different, and I hated
that. I wanted to be a boy just the same as my friends, not set
apart because my Dad was a clergyman. Since my Dad didn't
dress differently from other men, I thought I could try to hide
his occupation from my male friends. As I grew in stature, if
not in wisdom, the fact of Dad's difference became known to
my compatriots, and I hated it.

I have previously told of one of those defining events in the
development of this feeling, the day I arrived for school late
because of the horse trough "incident," and irrational as it was,
I determined early on, that if there was one thing I would never
be, it was a minister. I didn't reject my father or religion in any
way. I loved my father dearly and I always went to Sunday
School and church. I played my violin when Dad preached at St.
Elizabeth's Hospital or the Lutheran Home for the Aged, or at
the Gospel Mission. For me to follow in his footsteps, however,
was anathema.

Religion played a central part in our family life. Every morning, after breakfast, Dad would conduct family prayers. Sis and I always had a mad scramble for "Mama's lap," as Dad took down the family Bible from its place atop the china closet and read to us from its condensed wisdom of the ages. As little tots, Mother's loving embrace and Dad's quiet reading made everything all right.

After Dad read from the Bible, we would all get down on our knees while Dad prayed, seemingly unceasingly. As Sis and I grew up and and were going to school, another dimension began to enter the picture. Some of our classmates would stop by to accompany us to school. My sister would invite her friends in, but for me, it was too sissified to be down on my knees in prayer. When my friends came by, I went to the door, told them that we were at prayers and left them outside.

This didn't work with some of my friends, especially Meigs. He would barge in anyway and sit with us through prayers. To make matters worse, he started coming earlier and more regularly to hear Dad read from the Bible. This was really *de trop*. Why did he have to come anyway? He already knew my father was a preacher; he knew my father was *different*. Why did he have to rub it in?

When the time came for me to go to college, I wanted to follow my idol, Bill Mengert, to Haverford College. It was a Quaker school, not a Lutheran institution, such as Gettysburg, where many of Dad's friends thought I should go. Haverford, however, was an excellent school and the folks agreed that I could go there. In college, I majored in the social sciences, economics, and sociology. There was little religion in my college studies. I did, however go to Philadelphia to teach a Sunday School class in a Quaker settlement house.

On graduation, I won a fellowship in economics at Brown and another in family casework at Western Reserve University. Social work had a strong appeal to me, not wishy-washy sentimentality, but applied Christianity, so off to Cleveland I went in the fall of 1931. As part of my studies, I worked for Associated

Charities as a family caseworker. This was before the New Deal with its "alphabet soup" of social programs and agencies. I was supposed to help adjust maladjusted individuals to their environment. The environment, however, was so maladjusted that our hands were tied. The Community Chest, which raised money for a wide group of charities including ours, set its budget at $12 million. Men who had been out of work for a year were called back for a day and their wages given to the Community Chest. Still, the chest failed.

Associated Charities was simply swamped. We had so little money we could only give a family of five $3.50 a week for food; a single man was only given a dollar. I looked at myself. How could I hand a man one dollar a week, when I had so much? It wasn't that I was rich, but compared to others, my life looked pretty good. As a student, I lived in a boarding house that catered to students. We called our landlady, "The Mrs." I paid $10 a month for my room and an additional $.50 a week for kitchen privileges. Food, however, was not included, and I soon tired of the various beans with rice and rice with beans combinations. It became ghastly. How I longed for my mother's cooking.

One day the uncle of one of my fellow lodgers came to town and took half a dozen of us to Child's restaurant on Sunday noon for dinner. Our benefactor was Dr. Jerome Davis, a Professor of Practical Philanthropy at Yale Divinity School. Child's had a sign in the window, "All you can eat—$.60," and like a plague of devouring locusts, we descended on the eatery and gorged ourselves. After dinner, Professor Davis delivered a lecture on the Cleveland Town Hall Program. I was enraptured. Here was a man who made religion real. There was nothing "sissified" about him. I was so impressed that I quit the impossible job of being a social worker and arranged to go to Yale to study social ethics under Dr. Davis. After everything I had said, I was on my way to becoming a minister.

My conversion to becoming a clergyman was still far from complete. I was still so uncomfortable with my choice that I told my folks that I was going to Yale Graduate School.

That was true, but only half true. Yale Divinity School was indeed one of Yale's graduate schools, but not *the* Graduate School. As time went on, I became more comfortable. I began to see what real religion meant. For me, theology could be reduced to a simple axiom: the fatherhood of God, and the brotherhood of man. I was interested in the religion *of* Jesus, not the religion *about* Jesus. I soon rid myself of my foolish childhood misconceptions about ministers and religion, and decided to become a Methodist minister. My young life had come full circle.

A half-century after graduating from Eastern High School, I came back to Washington for my class' fiftieth anniversary reunion. We came back from all over America. I came from my farm in Vermont. Meigs, my boyhood friend, came up from Florida. Others came from the West, Midwest, and South. Meigs and I stayed at the same hotel, and over breakfast together, we reminisced about our long lost youth. Files stored away in the recesses of my mind came floating up to my consciousness. After some time, Meigs turned to me and said, "George, your father was the best man I ever knew."

I was flabbergasted. Why would Meigs say a thing like that? My brain raced through our boyhood years, as memory collapsed time. Meigs continued, "Remember how I used to come to your house on my way to school?"

"I sure do," I replied, "and I was never so mortified in my life as when you came in and saw me at family prayers on my knees."

"Why do you think I came?" countered Meigs.

Slowly the truth dawned on me, and I blurted out, "Do you mean that you deliberately came so as to be part of our family prayers?"

"Yes," he said, "I didn't get anything like it at my house, and when I saw what your father was doing, I wanted more. That's why I came every morning."

My mind was a whirl. A kaleidoscope of events from my early life rushed into my consciousness. I remembered "Pop" Kerper and the horse trough. I remembered my second-grade teacher passing out cards requesting "father's occupation" and leaving it blank. I remembered Dad's elderly lady parishioners asking me if I wanted to become a preacher like my father. Most of all, however, I remembered my childish shame that my father was somehow different from other boy's fathers.

Ruminating over my conversation with Meigs, as my wife and I drove home to Vermont, the truth hit me squarely between the eyes. As a child, I had been ashamed of the best man I had ever known. How stupid could I have been? Meigs saw it. My other friend, "Skin Dirty," when he would come to the door and ask if my "brother" was home, intuitively recognized what I had missed. He was of course referring to my father. His father was a drunk, and "Skin Dirty" could not conceive of a father spending time with his son. Suddenly the teachings of Halford Luccock, the great professor of homiletics came to me. I was the living example of what he taught—I had been ashamed, not of my worst, but of the best man I had ever known.

I was not alone in this failing. In fact, I had powerful company. Sir Arthur Conan Doyle, failing to recognize the marvel of his greatest creation, Sherlock Holmes, grew so unhappy with his character that he tried to kill him off. The public wouldn't have it. Similarly, Beatrix Potter, creator of the much beloved *Peter Rabbit* stories became so sick of rabbits that she spent her last years shooting them. Likewise, Simon Peter in the Bible story did the same thing. Before the crucifixion, he denied Christ.

As I look back on those halcyon days of childhood, I thank God for the "simpler times" I grew up in, and most of all for the finest father a boy could have. Thanks be to Him that I finally woke up and stopped being ashamed of my best. Now in my 88th year, I look back with great satisfaction and pride at the rewards of many years of following in my father and grandfather's footsteps in serving God and my fellow man.

Index